GOD'S PROFITS

GOD'S PROFITS

Faith, Fraud, and the Republican Crusade for Values Voters

SARAH POSNER

Foreword by
JOE CONASON

PoliPointPress

God's Profits: Faith, Fraud, and the Republican Crusade for Values Voters

Copyright © 2008 by Sarah Posner
All rights reserved, including the right to reproduction in whole, in part, or in any form.

Portions of this book appeared in a slightly different form in *The American Prospect:* "Pastor Strangelove," July 6, 2006, and "With God on His Side," November 10, 2005. *The American Prospect,* 2000 L Street NW, Suite 717, Washington, DC 20036. All rights reserved.

Production management: BookMatters
Book Design: BookMatters
Cover Design: Jeff Kenyon

Library of Congress Cataloging-in-Publication Data

Posner, Sarah.
    God's profits : faith, fraud, and the Republican crusade for values voters / Sarah Posner ; foreword by Joe Conason.
        p.   cm.
Includes bibliographical references and index.
ISBN 0-9794822-1-6 (alk. paper)
    1. Republican Party (U.S. : 1854–)   2. Evangelicalism–United States.   3. Fundamentalism–United States.   4. Christianity and politics–United States.   5. Faith movement (Hagin)–United States.   I. Title.
JK2356.P73   2008
324.2734–dc22   2007042123

Published by:
PoliPointPress, LLC
P.O. Box 3008
Sausalito, CA 94966–3008
(415) 339–4100
www.p3books.com

Distributed by Ingram Publisher Services

For Nate
because it all matters

Touch not mine anointed,
and do my prophets no harm.

—PSALM 105:15

Those who dare to question or criticize Word
of Faith teachers may find themselves publicly
rebuked or even anathematized. . . . This sort
of "spiritual intimidation" is justified by reference
to Psalm 105:15.

—ANDREW PERRIMAN, ed.,
Faith, Health and Prosperity

Contents

Foreword

JOE CONASON

Among the most remarkable features of religious fundamentalism in America is the resilience of the flock, whose loyalty has so often been tested in recent decades by public exposure of their shepherds as hypocrites, charlatans, and crooks. Ostentatious piety is obviously no hindrance to financial chicanery, substance abuse, or the many varieties of sexual misconduct attributed to ranking figures in the evangelical leadership. The steady accumulation of embarrassments would suggest that many televangelists and megachurch pastors are less sincere than the typical bookie or used-car salesman.

And yet even the most dishonest and abusive of them not only survive but continue to thrive, growing in wealth and influence while spawning dozens of imitators.

There is, of course, nothing new about the swindling preacher, long a stock character American folklore and fiction. Over the past fifty years television has transformed these traditional knaves into a phalanx of corporate media executives who command the attention of millions nationwide and even around the world.

Once upon a time, the nation was truly scandalized by the sexual peccadilloes of Jimmy Swaggart, the Louisiana televangelist who regularly patronized prostitutes, and James Bakker, whose extramarital affairs were less troubling than the business flimflams that eventually sent him to prison. More than two decades later, was anybody shocked to hear that Ted Haggard, pastor of a huge congregation and former president of the National Association of Evangelicals, had used narcotics with a male prostitute?

Such episodes may demonstrate nothing more than the eternal weakness of humanity, as the televangelists themselves would assure us. But beyond the tabloid stories of sin and repentance lies much evidence of systemic cynicism on the religious right.

It would be difficult to imagine a story more disillusioning than that of Ralph Reed, who symbolized the yearnings of millions of conservative evangelicals as the founding organizer of the Christian Coalition. At the zenith of the Christian Coalition's power, Reed abandoned the organization, which soon sank amid troubles with the Internal Revenue Service and petty internecine feuding. Reed went on to become a political consultant and earned millions by selling his services and religious credibility to casino operators, while still pretending to oppose gambling as a good Christian. The youthful Reed, whose choirboy looks concealed a cheating heart, belonged to the infamous lobbying ring that included Tom DeLay, the former House majority leader who resigned under a cloud of indictment and investigation, and Ed Buckham, a pastor who served as DeLay's "spiritual adviser."

Even as he and his cronies stank up Capitol Hill with their moral rot, DeLay continued to insist that God "is using me, all the time, everywhere, to stand up for biblical worldview in everything that I do and everywhere I am. He is training me, He is working with me." Sincerely religious people might wonder what God told DeLay and his pious pals about those lavish corporate-funded trips and dinners and donations—and about the tens of thousands of dollars funneled to DeLay's wife. The actual Bible is quite clear on such questions, according to Exodus 23:8 and Job 36:18, which specifically warns: "Be careful that no one entices you by riches; do not let a large bribe turn you aside."

What Sarah Posner shows in this disturbing and meticulously reported book is that such scriptural injunctions are simply irrelevant to a large and growing subculture of Christian evangelicalism known as "Word of Faith." Over the past twenty years, the Word of Faith movement has achieved explosive growth, not only among white evangelicals in the South but across racial and geographical divides. Preaching the "prosperity gospel" or the "health and wealth gospel," the movement's exponents claim to be able to heal the sick and bring affluence to the poor—if only the believers tithe and obey as demanded by its preachers.

Many Christian leaders, whether mainline or evangelical, regard these promises as arrant superstition or even heresy, but the Word of Faith movement is continually expanding—and its rising stars have gained more than a measure of respectability. Money-grubbing, authoritarian, and plagued by scandal, they nevertheless seem invulnerable to doubt. Their followers live in a strange subculture of "Hebraic Christianity," end-times prophecy, and constant pressure to send in more money in the hope of healing cancer and saving mortgages from foreclosure. They dismiss negative news reports concerning the lavish lifestyles and dubious conduct of their preachers as works of Satan.

The bamboozling of hopeful rubes is often sad and always fascinating. But the quasi-religious scams of today's evangelicals might be no more worrisome than mail-order impotence cures or penny-stock frauds, except for one salient difference: the political clout wielded by Word of Faith preachers such as Rod Parsley, who bills himself as a "Christocrat" and boasts of his connections in the White House and at the highest levels of the Republican Party.

Not so long ago, Republican leaders would have shunned a man like Parsley, who barks and grimaces and struts onstage, pretending to cure sickness and constantly demanding pledges of money from his working-class Ohio parishioners. The reputable businessmen and lawyers who led the Grand Old Party would have blanched at the sight of a Christian minister peddling "covenant swords" and "prayer cloths" to the poor, sick, and elderly, with the promise that these trin-

kets can cure asthma and pay off credit cards. They would have re-
garded any association with such a mountebank as shameful and
would have abhorred any reliance on him for electoral success as a
gross betrayal of the party of Abraham Lincoln, Theodore Roosevelt,
and Dwight Eisenhower.

But those gentlemen and their sense of dignity have long since
disappeared from the Republican ranks. Although respectable corporate types still finance the party, it is ruthless operatives such as
Karl Rove who shape its alliances and strategies. Rove undoubtedly
admires the authoritarian style of the Word of Faith preachers, especially if their commands produce obedient voters on Election Day.

Moreover, as Posner explains in detail, the political dogma of the
Word of Faith movement is entirely congruent with the antigovernment attitudes of the Republican right. If faithful tithing can ensure
good health and abundant wealth, then why would any obedient believer need Social Security, Medicare, or unemployment insurance?
And if there is one thing that the Word of Faith preachers dislike
about big government, it is law enforcement officers snooping into
how they run their "charities" and how they take advantage of their
religious tax exemptions.

Conservative organizer and lobbyist Grover Norquist once declared that the Republican Party represented the "leave-us-alone
coalition," and there is nothing that Rod Parsley would like more
than to be left alone by government and the media, to victimize his
gullible parishioners without interference by anyone. The Word of
Faith gospel is, as Posner writes, "the ultimate in laissez-faire capitalism, regulated only by God"—who speaks through the preachers, of
course.

Like all right-wing demagogues, the Word of Faith preachers
loudly proclaim their patriotism—and increasingly promote war
against Islam as the biblical purpose of the United States, another urgent topic that Posner explores in these pages. Back when George W.
Bush was still popular, they colluded in promoting the notion that

his presidency was divinely ordained, that he receives divine guidance, and that he is fulfilling the nation's destiny according to the will of the Almighty. Such assurances could come only from preachers who had themselves been chosen by God to transmit the dictates of heaven.

The nation's founders, however, rightly rejected the submission of the people to religious dictates—from any pulpit—as antithetical to liberty and a danger to the republic. The founders understood that any sovereign accountable to nobody but God was incompatible with democracy and constitutional order. What was true for the crowned heads of Europe two hundred years ago is equally true for the "anointed" heads of central Ohio today.

In these pages, Posner shows us the underside of the evangelical right—irrational, avaricious, xenophobic, exploitative, and hostile to freedom. It is a portrait that many Americans have never seen, and it requires a long, hard look from all of us.

Introduction

The first time I saw Rod Parsley in person he was on his *Silent No More* book tour in Washington, D.C., in April 2005. I was on assignment for *American Prospect* magazine to cover Parsley and, in particular, the white televangelist's efforts to court black Republican voters. Although I had seen Parsley on television and had read a smattering of news coverage on his vitriolic support for Ohio's 2004 gay marriage ban, I did not really know what to expect, either of the audience in liberal Washington or of the reactionary preacher when he stood on what must be one of the most Democratic pieces of real estate in the country. So when Parsley came charging onto the stage in Washington's storied Constitutional Hall and declared that "the devil will not be joining us tonight," I saw not just a clever political operative, or even just a political operative used, as most religious leaders are, by Republicans to garner the so-called values voters. I saw instead a neo-Pentecostal preacher with enough fire, brimstone, sweat, and spit to pack megachurches and revivals across the country. Parsley is not courted for his political acumen. He is not courted for his insightful prescriptions for solving society's ills. He is not even courted for his wisdom on the Scriptures. Parsley is put on stage because he is an entertainer.

Parsley is a man of many talents: he claims to incite revolutions and revivals, to heal homosexuality, to erase debt, to make troubled marriages whole, to make diabetes go away. He'll pray and weep and cast out devils and speak in tongues and slay people in the Holy Spirit and remind you that he is not a Republican or a Democrat but a "Christocrat." He leads a twelve-thousand-member church, a school that runs from preschool through college, a ministerial fellowship with two thousand members, and two political organizations, the Center for Moral Clarity and Reformation Ohio. He lives in a 7,500-square-foot million-dollar house shielded from view by a wall of evergreen trees and protected from intruders by an iron security fence manned by a guard. He'll never stop reminding you how busy he is preaching the Gospel—so busy, in fact, that he needed his church to buy him his own private airplane to enable him to do that. God talks to him. He obeys God. He therefore expects you to obey him.

He commanded his Washington audience to buy his book and urged them to give the DVD that accompanies it to their friends "because I cannot be explained, I can only be experienced." I, too, was about to experience Rod Parsley, and the world of religious television that he inhabits, a public world of big money and political drama but also a private world of people's dreams for spiritual and material fulfillment. When religion and politics collide, the result is explosive. When religion and politics collide with money and personal ambition, the result is toxic.

Parsley preaches a brand of Christianity that has been shaped by a religious movement called Word of Faith, which emphasizes the power of the born-again believer in Jesus Christ to call things into existence, including the believer's own physical and mental health and, most important, the believer's financial prosperity. Because of its emphasis on the believer's divine right to physical well-being and financial riches, Word of Faith is often called the "prosperity gospel" or the "health and wealth gospel." As a movement, not a denomination, Word of Faith has no membership or doctrinal requirements, but its tenets have become embedded in the late-twentieth-century nondenominational Pentecostal movement known as neo-Pentecostalism.

"If one theme can surmise neo-Pentecostalism," writes Tulane University sociologist Shayne Lee, "it is the emphasis on the role of the Holy Spirit to empower Christians to live with health, vitality, prosperity, and productivity."[1] Yet while it presents itself as a benign message of hope and purpose, critics of Word of Faith charge that it is a heresy that robs its followers of spiritual fulfillment, an affinity fraud that robs them of their money, and a distortion of the Scriptures, run by authoritarian preachers who rob their followers of their autonomy.

Politically, Word of Faith is an essentially conservative movement that benefits from conservative policies. Conservative evangelicals generally are opposed to abortion, homosexuality, pornography, and the separation of church and state—the bedrock of the so-called values voters. But followers of Word of Faith also preach an economic message that is inherently conservative. The prosperity gospel doesn't need regulation or legislation. A believer doesn't need the government to regulate corporations. If you don't make enough money, it's your own fault for not believing enough, for not speaking the word, for not claiming what is divinely yours. A believer doesn't need a government safety net if things go wrong. As Parsley says, "The best thing government can do to help the poor is to get out of the way. If government reduced taxes, removed industrial restraints, eliminated wage controls, and abolished subsidies, tariff[s], and other constraints on free enterprise, the poor would be helped in a way that [Aid to Families with Dependent Children], Social Security, and unemployment insurance could never match."[2] Of course he wants his followers to believe they can get out of poverty by believing in his message. His gospel is the ultimate laissez-faire capitalism, regulated only by the invisible hand of God.

As they look ahead to the 2008 presidential election and beyond, most political observers are debating what role the "evangelical vote" will play in the campaign. That conservative, politicized evangelicals—of which the Word of Faith movement is an increasingly significant part—are a permanent fixture in American politics is undeniable. They have a savvy, far-reaching political operation that calls its followers not just to the voting booth but to grassroots activism and political service at the federal, state, and local levels. They have had their political obituary written more than once, but they have always reemerged, fierce and determined, and will continue to play their hand as long as candidates and their consultants believe they need their followers' votes to win.

To be sure, much of the country is disgusted by and weary of the authoritarian Puritanism that pervades the rhetoric of the religious right: its relentless moralizing; its homophobia; its shameless accusations of a secular plot against it; its disdain for tolerance and diversity and equal rights; its contempt for the constitutionally mandated separation of church and state; its calls for world-ending wars; its rejection of government good works, unless performed in the name of Jesus. But it would be a mistake to see the movement as just one-dimensional or static. As the prosperity message plays a growing role in evangelical churches, in Christian television, and in the popular culture, the conservative evangelical movement is evolving beyond the standard vitriol against abortion and homosexuality. This role of the prosperity preachers shows how the evangelical alliance with the conservative movement and the Republican Party is both flexible and formidable.

This book is about televangelists who have explicitly embraced Word of Faith teachings, marketed their ability to create miraculous health and wealth in their followers' lives, and created authoritarian church structures to maintain control over their congregations. This book is not an assessment (or an indictment) of the charismatic movement as a whole. Although many Word of Faith adherents identify themselves as "charismatic," charismatic Christianity is a much broader movement that includes Catholics, Pentecostals, and mainline Protestants who engage in glossolalia (speaking in tongues), prophesying, or faith healing but who have not necessarily embraced the prosperity gospel.[3] Although the number of followers of the prosperity gospel remains undocumented, in the U.S. more than a quarter of Protestants are charismatic or Pentecostal, and nearly one in five of all Americans are. Many of those have embraced the prosperity message; nearly half of all Christians in the United States agreed with the statement that "God will grant material prosperity to all believers who have enough faith," and those numbers are even higher among charismatics/Pentecostals.[4]

The prosperity message is increasingly featured not only in independent churches but also over the airwaves and on bookshelves. Prosperity preachers like Joel Osteen, Joyce Meyer, and T. D. Jakes have become best-selling authors, with prized positions on display at mainstream bookstores. Its followers are diverse, racially and economically. Its churches are in the Bible Belt and in urban centers on both coasts. The prosperity gospel, considered by many to be an antireligion, has become a pervasive feature of American Christianity and culture. And because of the ambition of many of its most prominent proponents—who are considered by their followers to be prophets and apostles its leaders have increasingly been embraced by vote-hungry politicians and their calculating advisers.

Many books have ably chronicled the ascendancy of the Christian right in Republican politics, but none have identified the prosperity movement as the party's natural ally or as a growing force within the Christian right. This book will show how Republicans have reached out to major leaders within the prosperity movement as a way of diversifying the party's evangelical base beyond traditional (and mostly white) denominations like the Southern Baptist Convention and Pentecostal denominations like the Assemblies of God. In the pews of nondenominational churches that preach the prosperity message and in the audiences of prosperity televangelists, Republicans find racially diverse, socially conservative believers who are also receptive to economic conservatism. In their leaders' conspicuous wealth, accumulated through followers' donations, believers see proof that God, not policy, is the driving force of prosperity. The Republican alliance with the prosperity movement—touted as a shared love of God—is actually about something even more sacred: money.

ONE

A Marriage Made in Heaven

Government welfare is a distortion and a deception
from Satan. By allowing the government to take our
place, Christians have ceded our best chance to live
the gospel before our friends, neighbors, and family.
— JOHN HAGEE, endorsing George W. Bush
for president in 2000

Inside the Trinity Christian Church in Irving, Texas, a crowd starts
gathering in the afternoon for a Victory Healing and Miracle Service
that is to begin at 7 p.m. that evening. People have traveled from as
far away as Ohio and Arkansas and Georgia to participate. Most are
waiting in the perimeter lobby of the church, camping out with pil-
lows and Bibles, ordering pizza, and waiting for an event that has
been hyped on Christian television for months. I approach one
woman, an African American member of televangelist Rod Parsley's
World Harvest Church in Columbus, Ohio. Judging from her
clothes, the woman could scarcely afford the plane ticket she bought
to see a performance of the preaching phenomenon whose services
she can attend three times a week at home in Columbus. She's almost in a trance, barely able to focus on me or what I am asking her,
and she brushes me aside as I inquire about her journey. People are
waiting to see healings and miracles; Parsley claims a quarter of a
million people have mailed in prayer cloths (and money) so that he
could put his "anointing" on them. Once returned to the donor, the
prayer cloths can be used to heal anything in a broken life, from depression to cancer to joblessness to debt.

Trinity Christian Church is owned by the Trinity Broadcasting Network (TBN), the largest Christian television network in the world, and is on the grounds of the Irving outpost of the Orange County, California–based conglomerate that monopolizes the Christian airwaves with its Word of Faith message of health and wealth. Also on the church grounds is a television studio inside a gaudy white building loaded with antiques purchased by TBN's co-owner, Jan Crouch. A plantation-style mansion with manicured grounds offers visitors a walk along a re-creation of the Via Dolorosa. But today all the employees are breathlessly preparing for Parsley's service, and I am brusquely denied the opportunity to take that walk. In the television studios, equipped to accommodate the set of a creationist program depicting humans living alongside dinosaurs, phone banks wait to receive calls asking for prayers and donating money. TBN is a nonprofit, and all those donations are tax-free to the organization, which pays the Crouches close to a million dollars a year and provides them countless other perks, including expense accounts, real estate in five states, luxury cars, and a private jet.

The Crouches have recently turned over Trinity Christian Church to Larry Huch, a televangelist from Portland, Oregon, who specializes in breaking "generational curses." (That night, Huch would claim to break the generational curse of poverty.) Although TBN still owns the building, Huch pastors it under the mantle of his "New Beginnings" trademark from Portland. Huch is a Hebraic Christian who wears a tallit (a Jewish prayer shawl) and yarmulke during his church services (although not during Parsley's service) and maintains a tzedakah box at the church. Hebraic Christians seek to return to their "Jewish roots" in preparation for the end of days, when they believe Christ will rise again over Jerusalem. On the walls of the lobby are photographs of Huch and several Texas members of Christians United for Israel (CUFI) with several members of the Texas congressional delegation, including Republican senators Kay Bailey Hutchison and John Cornyn, on the steps of the nation's

Capitol. CUFI is a lobbying group led by John Hagee, the San Antonio televangelist; the group claims to support Israel but advocates a conflagration at Armageddon at which non-Christians will be converted or die as Christ arrives for the Second Coming. The connections are widespread; Parsley is a regional director for CUFI, and tonight he, too, will make sacred objects his personal talisman as part of this elaborate fund-raising stunt.

It is an honor for Huch to host Parsley at his church. Parsley has emerged as a leading figure in Christian conservative politics and is a frequent visitor to the Bush White House and Capitol Hill. Many credit him with the GOP victory in his native Ohio in 2004, a result that gave Bush the necessary electoral votes to capture the White House a second time. Although Parsley was well-known in Word of Faith circles for years from his church and his television program, *Breakthrough*, he became a nationally recognized name in 2004 for his relentless campaigning for Ohio's gay marriage ban with Ohio's secretary of state and the Bush-Cheney reelection co-chair, Ken Blackwell. Huch is undoubtedly acting at the behest of his benefactors, the Crouches, who have arranged to have Parsley's service broadcast worldwide on TBN's flagship program, *Praise the Lord.*

Well before the service is scheduled to start, the church sanctuary fills up. The best seats are reserved for pastors affiliated with Parsley's franchise, the World Harvest Church Ministerial Fellowship. Soon church employees are shuttling people to overflow rooms inside the TBN studios a couple of parking lots away. I am crammed to the point of immobility in an upper-balcony pew of the four-thousand-seat sanctuary. The praise and worship bands are louder than I've ever experienced at any Word of Faith service, hyping the crowd into a frenzy and making it impossible to talk to anyone around me. People are dancing and singing, reaching their arms out toward the stage and holding their palms cupped upward, all set to receive the anointing. My ears are ringing as more people try to squeeze into the pews; no one objects except an elderly woman sitting next to me, who is angry about how loud it is. "Do they think God is deaf?" she demands over the thundering crowd. Soon she and her companion leave. Their spaces are quickly filled by people who had been sitting in the aisles.

The overamplified pop music of the Crabb Family, a band frequently featured on TBN programming, is nothing compared to the collective shriek of thousands of whistles that Parsley's assistants pass out in buckets. The whistles, it turns out, are surrogate shofars (the ram's horn blown in synagogues on high holidays) because, Parsley tells us, he couldn't find actual shofars. Parsley has a real shofar for himself, and after he blows it, he anoints himself the arbiter identified in the Gospel of Luke who will announce Jubilee. It's Jubilee, Parsley says with his characteristic absence of humility, "when the prophetic voice announces it. And I'm here to tell you, it's Jubilee." As pandemonium breaks out in the crowd, Parsley continues: "It's time for a perpetual party. Your long face is out of order. Your depression has got to go. . . . No more quiet services, mundane Christianity has got to go. Shout it, it's Jubilee!" He implores his audience to blow their whistles, which he claims can miraculously heal; he proclaims, "All tumors, swallowing problems, and cataracts are healed as people blow the whistles."

As strains of the familiar lead-in music for *Praise the Lord* are heard, along with the game-show-style announcement of "the world's largest prayer and praise gathering," the crowd roars its approval. Parsley, of course, pays homage to his TBN patrons, calling the network "the greatest soul-winning station in the world," and adding, "Let's thank God for Paul and Jan for making this night possible. We love you." The Crouches, who first hosted Parsley on *Praise the Lord* in 1983, when he was only twenty-six years old, have long placed their imprimatur on Parsley, too; in TBN's September 2000 newsletter, a photograph of Parsley bore the caption of Luke 10:19 ("I have given you authority over all the power of the Enemy") and proclaimed Parsley a prophet who "challenged God's people to

break through beyond status quo Christianity—invade enemy terri-
tory and overthrow the kingdom of darkness."[1] Parsley recounts that
Jan Crouch had "something wrong with her throat for years and
God gave her a tremendous healing" after she used one of Parsley's
prayer cloths.

Over the course of the evening, Parsley will slay people in the
Holy Spirit, lay hands on them, and profess to heal their cancer, homosexuality, and financial problems. He will walk over the pews as
people sway and fall to the floor. He will take credit for a woman's
new job as a marketing and database manager, which she says she
got after she sent Parsley her last $6. (Although her statement is
staged to look spontaneous, she had appeared on Parsley's television
program with an identical testimony a few weeks before.) Tonight he
will blow on her, and she will fall on the stage. He will claim, with
two members of his congregation as his witnesses, that he cured
their adopted baby who was born without a brain. "His head was
the size of his shoulders, nothing but water in that globe," Parsley
boasts. "They brought him into service, we laid hands on him. The
six o'clock news carried it; the eleven o'clock news carried it. Here
are the brain scans. Here's the child with no brain. Here is the child
after the prayer with a fully developed, completely normal function-
ing brain."[2]

Anne Gimenez, a televangelist from Virginia Beach, Virginia, is
called to the stage from the front pew. Parsley claims that she and
her husband, John, have "lost" hundreds of thousands of dollars
"shaking up" Washington, D.C. He doesn't explain it, but the
Gimenezes run America for Jesus, an organization whose board includes Parsley and other luminaries from the Word of Faith world.
America for Jesus has organized over two hundred political prayer
rallies. John Gimenez has taken credit for the election of Ronald
Reagan with the 1980 National Mall rally, and he organized a rally
there in 2004 that was supportive of George W. Bush's reelection.[3]
Anne is holding Parsley's hand, but he tells her to switch to his other

hand because the anointing is coming out of that one. He claims she will receive seven times the money she "lost." Gimenez falls to the stage, where she lies for at least ten minutes. Parsley's handlers are laying hands on people in the front rows as others sing, dance, hop, raise their arms, and blow the whistles.

Parsley recognizes that for many people his faith healing doesn't quite jibe with his recently acquired—and carefully cultivated—status as a political player. In a relatively short time, Parsley has hoisted himself onto the national political stage. He has been named one of the fifty most influential Christians in America and one of the ten most influential GOP religious kingmakers shaping the 2008 race for the White House.[4] In a television broadcast a week before this service, Parsley claimed to be "the only preacher brave enough to be in the White House one day and praying over prayer cloths the next, casting out devils."[5] But his in-your-face attitude spills over into a nationally televised nose-thumbing at his critics, in which he showcases "revelation knowledge," a hallmark of Word of Faith preaching. As one Word of Faith follower told me, "That's all faith is, it's believing the word over what you see happening all around you, you know, circumstances. In a nutshell, that's what faith is. Believing the word instead of the circumstances."[6] As a result, scholarship, journalism, and other non-biblical pursuits of truth are derided.

Parsley, a Bible college dropout, notes that his political celebrity has mushroomed despite the efforts of skeptics. "Somebody said to me the other day, 'You are the strangest person I've ever seen. . . . One day you're in the halls of Congress and the next day you're shouting and screaming in other tongues and laying hands on prayer cloths.'" Parsley sneers at his imaginary critics. "That's because I don't determine my theology based on my experience. Don't let anybody back you down on truth. Don't let anybody stare over the brim of their glasses with a circle of smoke enwreathing their head. Don't let anybody sitting on a university or college campus or behind a news desk somewhere intimidate you from truth. Once you know you've got ahold of absolute truth, you let nothing turn your plow." The crowd cheers wildly, and people are speaking in tongues, but the din is eclipsed by the earsplitting screech of the whistles.

Free-Market Jesus

Parsley is not a lone ranger plucked from obscurity because of his political acumen to lead a new generation of evangelicals. Word of Faith proponents have long made comfortable bedfellows with conservatives and Republicans, despite the view of many conservative (and liberal) Christians that Word of Faith is a heretical distortion of the Bible. In their quest to nail down the evangelical vote, Republicans have long recognized that prosperity preachers—regardless of how outlandish or peculiar they might seem to mainline Christians—have huge followings and are therefore worth cultivating for votes. And because of·their followings, their television antics are overlooked, as is the unregulated environment in which they profit.

To understand exactly why Word of Faith is so compatible with Republican political and economic ideology, one need look no further than the central tenet of Word of Faith preaching: the so-called prosperity gospel. Word of Faith promises prosperity to believers and fuels churches that operate like closely held corporations. The high-living pastor and his family tightly control the money without accountability to congregants or the government. Under the Internal Revenue Code, churches do not pay taxes, nor are they required to file tax returns. Because of Internal Revenue Service (IRS) rules and the absence of any other legal requirements for transparency or accountability, the financial affairs of churches can legally be kept totally secret. Although many houses of worship voluntarily offer financial accountability to their donors, the leading Word of Faith churches do not. As a result, they can parlay their nonprofit status into multimillion-dollar enterprises, without outside scrutiny.

Although legally recognized as nonprofits, these churches are
driven by a divinely sanctioned profit motive. Making tithes and offerings to such a prosperous ministry demonstrates the giver's faith
in God and will result in a harvest of abundance in every facet of
life: health, finances, relationships, and spirituality. According to
Parsley, poverty is evidence of lack of faith in God. Government programs only get in the way; if people just had enough faith, they
wouldn't need a government safety net, because their poverty would
vanish. Parsley frequently decries the pervasiveness of poverty, but
his solutions have nothing to do with public policy and everything to
do with giving money to the church: "Your seed (tithes and offerings) has within itself the power of life. . . . I want you to realize that
the power to get wealth to set our society free is in the seed."[7] The
popular San Antonio televangelist John Hagee has called on his followers to "take America back . . . from a brain-dead government that
has produced a welfare state, taxing those who will work and giving
the money to those who can work but won't. That is contrary to the
word of God."[8]

The main tenets of Word of Faith are revelation knowledge,
through which the believer derives knowledge directly from God,
rather than from the senses; identification, through which the believer is inhabited by God and is another incarnation of Jesus; positive confession, or the power of the believer to call things into existence; the right of believers to divine health; and the right of
believers to divine wealth.[9] The believer, a "little god," is anointed
and therefore can reject reason in favor of revelation, a "higher
knowledge that contradicts the senses."[10] It is through revelation
knowledge that the Word of Faith movement has created its alternate
universe in which rational thought is rejected and where the media,
intellectual thought, science, and any type of critical thinking are
scorned. Drawing on the Pentecostal tradition of casting out devils,
pursuits associated with the Enlightenment are denounced as the
work of Satan.

Prosperity Gospel Thrives in the Reagan Era

Although Word of Faith—and particularly its promises of health and wealth—has permeated Pentecostalism and neo-Pentecostalism for decades, Word of Faith churches saw explosive growth during the Reagan era. Televangelist Robert Tilton once told his television audience that hearing Reagan talk about prosperity in America made him want to be a prosperity preacher.[11] In 1991, an investigation by leading televangelist watchdog Trinity Foundation and ABC's *Primetime Live* exposed the corrupt inner workings of Tilton's ministry, revealing practices that included taking money out of envelopes containing viewer prayer requests and throwing the prayer requests away. Exposed for unabashedly enriching himself on the proceeds, Tilton even lost his coveted airtime on TBN. One of Tilton's targets was African Americans,[12] who were increasingly drawn to Word of Faith during the 1980s. One of the few outlets to carry his program today is Black Entertainment Television.[13]

Sociologist Milmon F. Harrison, who has documented the increasing popularity of Word of Faith among African Americans, writes that "the harsh realities of Reagan era economic policies for the nation's most vulnerable were very different from what was being portrayed of American life by the mass entertainment media. Popular culture of the time seemed to be shaped by the mass media producers' obsession with glorifying consumption through many highly successful television programs." These programs included *Lifestyles of the Rich and Famous, Dynasty, Dallas, Falcon Crest, Miami Vice*, and the popular program that symbolized black upward mobility, *The Cosby Show*. According to Harrison, "the reality of life in many African-American families belied the Reagan administration's claims ... of unbridled upward mobility and access to wealth and prosperity for all who worked hard." As a result, Word of Faith offered "a shining hope and an answer to the question why some people (especially born-again Christians) were not prospering in the midst of so much wealth. The answer was that those people had not been taught what the Bible really says about wealth and who should possess it. What appeared to be impossible through mere hard work and the secular opportunity structure God's favor could make possible for believers who know who they are in Christ."[14]

The prosperity gospel is so pervasive that, according to Shayne Lee, the Tulane sociologist, "today it would be very difficult to find an African-American church with members unaffected by prosperity teachings."[15] Despite many black pastors' opposition to Word of Faith teaching, Lee says, their congregants are exposed to the teaching through television, conferences, books, and other media.[16] But the influence of Word of Faith is not limited to the black church. It has also permeated the preaching and teaching seen in white and Hispanic neo-Pentecostal or charismatic churches as well. Most Word of Faith congregations are racially diverse, with many of the white preachers attracting sizable black audiences.

It was no accident, then, that Word of Faith flourished in the "greed decade" of the Reagan era, providing a justification for wanting wealth and giving the word *entitlement* a new meaning. Believers are entitled to prosperity. No government safety net is required for true believers, who will be blessed with abundance for their faith in God. The Reverend Tony Lee, who pastors the Community of Hope African Methodist Episcopal Church in a poor, predominantly black area of Prince George's County, outside of Washington, D.C., critiques it as "a transaction-based kind of faith" that focuses people on themselves rather than on combating social and economic inequality in their communities. "God . . . is like an American Express account in which when you use it, you get points," Lee said. It places the focus on the individual rather than the community. Because people get very wrapped up in the preachers' or televangelists' personalities, Lee added, they believe "'I have to pay to be connected to you. So that I can get more connected to God.' And that's an extremely dangerous place to be. And that kind of atmosphere makes it much harder to try to mobilize people around social justice issues."[17] This, in turn, says Princeton University professor Melissa Harris-Lacewell, "has implications for the future of black politics. . . . There is some evidence that [prosperity preachers'] message dampens political activism among African Americans. This effect can have significant consequences for the Democratic Party, which relies heavily on African American turnout in local and national elections."[18]

Given the growth of Word of Faith teaching, it is also no surprise that Reagan's ambitious vice president, George H. W. Bush, although tone-deaf on evangelical issues, gratefully accepted the recommendation of a trusted adviser to reach out to Word of Faith pastors to bolster his credentials among evangelicals. In 1986, Doug Wead, then–Vice President Bush's religious liaison, compiled a list of one thousand "targets"—religious leaders ripe for being pandered to in election years because of their ability to draw in voters. Wead's advice to Bush—and to George W., who became Wead's boss on his father's presidential campaign—was not to put all his eggs in one basket.[19] Given the rising influence of Word of Faith, some of the movement's most prominent spokespeople became targets.

Bush Targets Prosperity Preachers

Wead stage-managed the stiff, Episcopalian vice president's religious conversion, which was undertaken in a hunt for votes. Wead has worked as an Amway distributor and motivational speaker and has been close, over the years, with leading evangelical figures, major funders of the conservative movement, and the power brokers of prosperity televangelism. He has come to televangelists' aid when they were disgraced, defending Tilton, faith healer Benny Hinn, and Crouch in the face of media scrutiny that exposed their corrupt practices. When acting as an adviser to both Bushes during their presidential campaigns, Wead simultaneously encouraged his bosses to cultivate the televangelists for votes while warning them of their controversial doctrine. But Wead fell out of favor with the Bushes in 2005 after he released portions of secretly taped telephone conversations with George W. Bush when he was governor of Texas, conversations in which Bush appeared to have admitted to smoking marijuana.

But back in the 1980s, during the spectacular growth of Word of Faith teaching, Wead provided George Herbert Walker Bush with a master plan for winning the White House with evangelical votes. After he rewrote a speech Bush subsequently delivered to rave reviews at the National Religious Broadcasters convention in 1985, Wead was entrusted with the job of religious liaison, a role he continued when George W. Bush came on as his boss during the 1988 presidential campaign. Wead advised Bush Sr. to use code language and expressions that would impress evangelicals without offending nonevangelicals. He offered to arrange for a cameraman to catch the vice president with a tear in his eye as he listened to the evangelist and Bush family friend Billy Graham preach. Wead recalled that the elder Bush said, "You know I'm a friend of Billy Graham's, and I don't want this used for political purposes." But according to Wead, George W. Bush "just kind of rolled his eyes and said 'By God, I would.'" Reading one of Wead's memos on leading Texas evangelicals, Bush told Wead, "God, I could win the governorship with this."[20]

In his memo about targets, Wead's purpose was to avoid what he called the high "negatives" of divisive figures like Jerry Falwell or Pat Robertson by "diluting" Bush's appearances with evangelicals with less-recognized and less-controversial figures, including black pastors.[21] Among the leading targets were Wead's friend Jim Bakker and Jimmy Swaggart, who were both later brought down by scandal.[22] Although he worried about Bush associating with them too closely, Wead also put Pat Robertson and Jerry Falwell in the top dozen.

Wead, who believes he has prospered by following the tenets of the prosperity gospel, didn't hesitate to include Word of Faith preachers on his list of targets. Included among the top twelve of "the vice

president's friends" was Kenneth Copeland, today the leading proponent of the Word of Faith message and TBN's top moneymaker.[23] In
1985, after Bush met with Copeland and his wife, Wead wrote that the
couple was "quite taken by their Springfield visit with the Vice-
President and appear to be openly sympathetic toward his candidacy."[24] Despite describing TBN head Paul Crouch as "an exaggera-
tion of the most bizarre manifestation of the peculiar evangelical
subculture," Wead included Crouch on a list of "spare tires," a dozen or
so "prominent leaders who could be cultivated in place of" the twelve
main targets.[25] To back up the targets and spare tires, Wead compiled
a deep bench of about a thousand "evangelical leaders of influence"
who could be called upon in smaller ways. That list included Word of
Faith proponents Parsley and his mentor Lester Sumrall; Anne
Gimenez; televangelist Marilyn Hickey; Kenneth Hagin, considered by
most to be the official founder of the Word of Faith movement; and
Frederick Price, at the time its leading black proponent. Earl Paulk,
who at the time of this writing is embroiled in a wide-ranging sex
scandal that has spanned forty years, was also on the list.[26] After his
election, George H. W. Bush named one of Paulk's outreach ministries
as one of the "thousand points of light" the same year that several
women from the congregation accused him of sexually abusing them.
Even Tilton made the list. Wead still defends Tilton, whom he invited
to serve on the board of a private Christian school he heads. Wead
believes that Tilton "got screwed" by the *Primetime Live* story and
insists, contrary to what *Primetime* showed, that Tilton threw away the
prayer requests and the money in the envelopes.[27] Bush's 1988 presidential campaign employed the same direct-mail firm that Tilton used
to fleece his donors.[28]

Wead helped Bush craft another speech to the National Religious
Broadcasters meeting in 1987. That speech thrilled Crouch, who re-
broadcast portions of it on TBN. Crouch repeatedly sought to have
the vice president as a guest on TBN, which Wead advised Bush to
avoid because of the risk of alienating mainline Christians. Yet just

before the Super Tuesday primaries in 1988, Crouch broadcast a
carefully staged "interview" of the vice president by Wead himself,
deceptively identified as "correspondent Doug Wead." It consisted of
twenty-five minutes of softball questions intended to verify Bush's
commitment to his savior, Jesus Christ. Wead's fawning campaign
biography of Bush, *George Bush: Man of Integrity*, contained a transcript of the interview.[29]

Elected with the help of 81 percent of the evangelical vote, according to Wead, Bush continued to reach out to the televangelist
world as part of his continued pandering to evangelicals. According
to Carlton Pearson—a popular black televangelist of the period
whose annual Azusa Conference in Tulsa, Oklahoma, helped launch
many prosperity preachers, most notably T. D. Jakes, to stardom—
Wead would invite evangelical leaders to the White House and say,
"'Do you want to see the file on you?'" His voice now laced with sar-
casm, Pearson added, "and that was pretty impressive. That he had a
file on me, it made me feel more important."[30] Wead once lamented
the fact that George W. Bush, while running for president, didn't
have a photograph taken of a meeting with Pearson, because Pearson
could have placed it in his newsletter, which reached a valuable target group for Bush.[31]

Pearson now looks back with a healthy dose of skepticism, noting
that it was a "smart and shrewd political move, but I understand
what's behind it now."[32] The point, of course, was to win elections,
and Wead recalled that some of the religious leaders "would just
light up like a light bulb and do all kinds of things for us, and that
was one of the factors of the great victory that Bush had in '88."[33]
But in 1992 Bush was stung by disenchanted evangelicals, who felt
abandoned by him once he took office. Just before the election,
Crouch said on TBN, "I don't know who I'm going to vote for. Ross
Perot even looks good."[34] After his father's loss in 1992, George W.
Bush was to learn that although he didn't want to be seen publicly
with Crouch, the television mogul's support was essential.

The Rise of the Self-Help Gurus

During the Clinton era, Word of Faith and prosperity gospel churches continued to flourish. Conferences promoting the preachers and their teachings proliferated, and a new generation of preachers was becoming well-known. The culture of celebrity was colliding with a religious world that was increasingly viewing spirituality as a commodity. Televangelists who were good at selling it were becoming very popular indeed.

Joel Osteen, the son of the successful televangelist John Osteen and a dropout from Oral Roberts University, took over his father's Houston ministry and rapidly became a sensation in the Christian world for his cotton-candy, feel-good, self-help style of preaching. Osteen—whose slogan is "Discover the champion in you"—outgrew the megachurch he inherited from his father and moved his forty-thousand-member congregation to the Compaq Center sports arena in 2005, after performing a $75 million renovation to the facility. His first service in the new venue drew politicians as diverse as Texas governor Rick Perry and then–House minority leader Nancy Pelosi. Osteen's brother, Justin, runs a consulting firm that designs compensation packages for preachers, and he has designed packages for Parsley and Jakes.[35]

While Osteen was creating his own saccharine empire, another Texan—this one transplanted from West Virginia—had been assiduously building a ministry focused on prosperity for himself and his followers. T. D. Jakes really caught the eye of politicians, Democrats and Republicans alike. Although today Jakes omits the casting out of devils and the heavy-handed give-to-prosper preaching, his earlier preaching was more focused on those traditional neo-Pentecostal themes. At his church, he avoids the ham-handed pressure for tithing, but he will appear at a TBN telethon begging for cash for the network, which provided him his first national television platform. Shayne Lee, who describes Jakes as simultaneously Machiavellian, shrewd, loyal, and inspiring, says, "Whether or not Jakes is a prosperity preacher is debatable. Whether he's been influenced by the prosperity gospel I don't think is debatable."[36]

It is the Jakeses and the Osteens that politicians of both major parties like to be seen with as they preach their own brand of prosperity, filled with cheery optimism and bromides for successful living. Bush, who has written that he has been "spellbound" by Jakes's preaching, gave the televangelist money after he sold the Texas Rangers.[37] Barack Obama is said to consult Jakes on a weekly basis and called him a "role model" of a Christian who puts his faith into social action.[38] And Al Gore visited his church during the 2000 campaign. Jakes, sitting atop a multimillion-dollar empire, is too savvy to risk his near-ambassador status by engaging in blatant partisan politicking in exchange for a photo opportunity in the White House Rose Garden.

Although these alliances have been building since the Reagan era, it is in the Bush era that the Word of Faith megachurch pastors have become more visible in the Republican fold. Their increased prominence is due in part to campaign strategists, who are constantly making adjustments to sweep more activists and voters into their circles. The alliance is not only strategic but comfortable: the Word of Faith movement presented itself to campaign bean counters as the next big generation of voters whose worldview lines up with conservatism even more precisely than that of the conservative white denominational evangelicals who trade on the bread-and-butter issues of abortion and gay marriage. In Word of Faith audiences, Republicans see a body of voters receptive to a worldview based on extreme individualism and unfettered capitalism, where glitzy multi-million-dollar preachers are role models for audiences given a divine stamp of approval for their own self-interested aspirations.

But while the feel-good, self-empowerment message Jakes and Osteen preach typifies modern life, the anachronistic world of Pentecostalism, in which satanic forces are in constant battle with the forces of God, is still the unifying principle of the neo-Pentecostal message. Therefore, in an election year when the chips are down and the troops need to be rallied, the GOP turns to the fire and brimstone.

Election 2000: "God's Candidate" versus Satan

Although today John Hagee has become well-known because of his agitation for an Armageddon war with Iran and for his embrace by neoconservatives and hawkish Jews, back in 2000 he was little known outside his neo-Pentecostal circles. But the younger Bush knew that the San Antonio televangelist had a large television audience, which Wead estimated at seven million strong. Wead had ghostwritten Hagee's 1997 conspiracy-theory book, *Day of Deception*, which claims to take "a probing look inside the United States government and expose blatant acts of deception designed to destroy democracy in America." Those "acts of deception," according to the book, were carried out by the Antichrist in his effort to install a "one-world order." Evidence of the one-world order, according to Hagee, includes "the Eastern Establishment," the United Nations, the National Education Association (NEA), the Council on Foreign Relations,[39] and the Illuminati, the imaginary, shadowy group of international financiers that has long been fodder for conspiracy theorists.[40] Hagee didn't mention that many Illuminati theorists believe in a connection between the Illuminati and the Yale secret society Skull and Bones, to which both Bushes belong. Nor did Hagee, who bills himself as a friend of the Jews, note that Illuminati conspiracies have often included anti-Semitic narratives about Jewish bankers.

In his 1988 campaign biography of Bush Sr., Wead sought to dispel conspiracies that the Bush family was behind the supposed one-world order.[41] But as a ghostwriter, Wead blamed his old boss for trying to bring about what Hagee believes is a satanic, demonic "new world order."[42] Just one year after penning Hagee's conspiracy-laden screed, Wead was pushing Governor Bush and Karl Rove to arrange meetings between the governor and the pastor, and the governor enlisted Hagee to recruit other pastors to sign on to the Bush campaign effort.[43]

Despite accusing Bush Sr. of collaboration with the Antichrist, Hagee delivered for George W. Bush in his 2000 book, *God's Candidate for America*. Even though his tax-exempt status forbids him from endorsing candidates, Hagee was unequivocal that Jesus would vote for George W. Bush. "If you are concerned about the sort of America your children and grandchildren will grow up within," Hagee wrote, "then you need to cast your vote for George W. Bush and the Republican Party."[44] *God's Candidate*, like *Day of Deception*, decries Satan's work through the United Nations and the NEA but omits references to a new world order created by international financiers and the "Eastern Establishment." Hagee continued to promote the book even after Bush took office,[45] and he wrote a prayer for the president in the post-2004 election edition of Stephen Mansfield's campaign biography, *The Faith of George W. Bush*.

But for the vitriolic preacher, it wasn't enough to endorse Bush; Hagee had to equate the opposition with evil incarnate. The Democratic Party, Hagee wrote, "is the home of those who advocate homosexuality, abortion, free-sex, unlimited handouts, maximum taxation, little freedom from government control, and toleration of drug use." The GOP, in contrast, "is the home of social conservatives who believe in the sanctity of life, hard work, clean moral living, limited government interference in our lives, minimum taxation, and a return to Bible-based societal values."[46] The book was published by his nonprofit Global Evangelism Television, which that year used tax-exempt donor money to pay Hagee nearly half a million dollars in salary and deferred compensation for sixteen hours of work a week. Hagee earned another $300,000 from his church.[47] But in keeping with the Word of Faith credo that poverty is evidence of insufficient faith, Hagee went on to depict welfare as satanic:

> Instead of faith, Satan offers fear; instead of commitment, Satan
> offers selfish promiscuity; instead of stable home lives, Satan
> offers multiple divorces. Instead of career and gainful employ-
> ment, Satan offers laziness and quick-money schemes and
> gambling. Instead of Christian charity, Satan offers a lifetime
> on the public dole. God's will for each man and woman is to
> have positive self-esteem; Satan wants each man, woman, and
> child to feel insignificant.[48]

Hagee offered up then-governor Bush's taxpayer-funded, "faith-
based initiative" as the best alternative to Satan.[49]

The Bush-Hagee alliance entailed a cognitive dissonance as so-
called compassionate conservatism collided with mean-spirited denunciations of demon possession. Hagee lauded the Republican
Contract with America, spearheaded by former House Speaker Newt
Gingrich, who later admitted that he was committing adultery while
pursuing the impeachment of Clinton. Nonetheless, Hagee invited
Gingrich to be the keynote speaker for his 2007 Christians United for
Israel Washington Summit. Mirroring the right-wing noise machine,
while also reflecting the anti-intellectualism of Word of Faith, Hagee
added that "the worldy-wise pseudo-sophisticates of the major news
media will always put a positive spin on stories involving pet liberal
issues while sneering at issues important to Christians and conservatives."[50] Just like Parsley's derision for journalists and academics,
Hagee's disdain for "pseudo-sophisticates" reflects the Word of Faith
view that revelation knowledge is superior to the other truth-seeking
pursuits and that any endeavor driven by critical thinking is to be not
only scorned but mistrusted as the work of the devil himself.

The Spare Tire Gets Pumped

Although designated a spare tire in 1985, Crouch was the only
Christian television station owner in Wead's target memo who remains standing today. Jim Bakker's PTL network was brought down

by his sexual and financial scandals, and Pat Robertson later sold his Christian Broadcasting Network to Fox while keeping his production company. Paul Crouch now boasts ownership of the world's largest religious television network. By the time George W. Bush embarked on his own run for president eleven years later, Crouch's empire, and the televangelists who profit from it, were ripe for the picking.

TBN has been on the air since 1972, when Paul and Jan Crouch purchased a broadcast station in Southern California. Since that time, it has expanded into the world's largest Christian network, with the Crouches buying up broadcast stations across the country and expanding into cable and satellite programming. Today, with assets exceeding $300 million, TBN reaches viewers in North and South America, Europe, Asia, and Africa with its very American health and wealth gospel. Programming includes the flagship *Praise the Lord* program, frequently hosted by TBN's celebrity televangelists and with guest appearances by Hollywood figures like Kirk Cameron, Stephen Baldwin, and Mr. T. The daily *Behind the Scenes* purports to be a recap of the day's news but is often free advertising for TBN's for-profit ventures, such as the film *One Night with the King*, which was produced by Gener8Xion Entertainment, a film company that is owned by the Crouches' son Matt and his wife, Laurie, and that the nonprofit has poured financing into. And each day the stable of televangelists—Rod Parsley, John Hagee, Kenneth Copeland, Benny Hinn, T. D. Jakes, Kenneth Hagin, Creflo Dollar, Eddie Long, and many others—pay TBN to peddle their prosperity gospel through its airwaves. (Often the televangelists plead for money on the grounds that airtime is very expensive, raising the question: if TBN's purported goal is spreading the Gospel throughout the world, why wouldn't it let these anointed ones use the airwaves at cost?) TBN has expanded its offerings to Spanish-speaking viewers through Enlace channel, to youth through its JCTV cable network, and to young children through its Smile of a Child network.

Wead advised the younger Bush and his top adviser, Karl Rove, that Crouch was "a bit outlandish" yet that he "offers many avenues of communication." Another selling point for cozying up to Crouch was the evangelist's close relationship with John Ashcroft, whom Bush saw as a key ally. Crouch often boasts that as a child, he attended the same Assemblies of God church as Ashcroft, and he offered to help Ashcroft with campaign fund-raising for his 2000 Senate run. Crouch prominently featured a photograph of himself shaking hands with Ashcroft at Bush's first inauguration in the TBN newsletter.[51] Gore's appearance at Jakes's church, said Wead, "shows that this Pentecostal thing is not a figment of my imagination but very real."[52]

But as Wead wrote to Rove in the heat of the campaign in the summer of 2000, Bush's reticence was causing Crouch to be "driven into the hands of Al Gore, reluctantly so." Wead warned in July 2000 that Gore supported a piece of cable legislation important to Crouch, and Crouch had invited him to appear on the network. "Maybe this is good," wrote Wead. "Maybe the story of Gore's pandering or instability will transcend the apparent support from the nation's largest religious broadcaster. Maybe the news will pick up on a Crouch scandal as some have been predicting since 1986. But if that doesn't happen, you are kissing away the largest religious television network in America for nothing. He wants to support you."[53]

Throughout the summer Wead fretted that a Gore appearance— even without an explicit endorsement from Crouch—could provide evangelicals with "an excuse to vote for Gore." The prospect of the Gore TBN appearance, Wead cautioned Bush, "is very, very bad."[54] But just two days later, after consulting with the televangelist and faith healer Benny Hinn, another friend of Wead's, Crouch decided to withdraw his invitation to Gore. Moreover, Wead wrote, Crouch and Hinn agreed that although they supported Bush, it would be bad strategy for him to appear publicly with any high-profile evangelical. "So there it is," read the Wead missive to Bush and Rove, "falling into your lap unsolicited. You have Crouch and you don't even have to be on his show!"[55]

Once Bush was elected, Crouch expressed his elation on TBN. When his friend Ashcroft became attorney general, Crouch rejoiced that now "Christians finally have an opportunity to *BLESS* America!" after years of "misinformation" about the separation of church and state.[56] After 9/11, Crouch implored his viewers to "keep the Attorney General and the President in your prayers during this difficult time in our nation's history. As God's people, we are commissioned to 'PRAY for kings and ALL OTHERS who are in authority, so we can LIVE IN PEACE and in quietness, in godliness and dignity. This is good and pleases God our Savior, for He wants EVERYONE to be SAVED and understand the TRUTH.'"[57]

Scandals involving televangelists on TBN's airwaves drew little notice from politicians during Bush's presidency, just as Tilton's disgrace during Bush Sr.'s tenure brought no regulation of either the televangelists' tax-exempt status or of their unsubstantiated claims of miracles in exchange for money. Two years into Bush's first term, *Dateline NBC* aired a scathing exposé of Hinn's ministry, showing his shameless peddling of false hope to the sick and infirm through his "healing crusades," which draw tens of thousands to arenas around the world. Using hidden cameras, the news program showed Hinn's ability to mesmerize his crowd—and convince them of miraculous "signs and wonders." Backstage, the network showed Hinn's staff counting buckets of money that the audience had given to the preacher, who at the time was building an extravagant ocean-view mansion in California. The donations were tax-free to Hinn's televangelism "church," which was paying for the construction of what Hinn's organization termed his "parsonage." Hinn denounced NBC on TBN with ominous warnings that the network had come against God's anointed. For a few years after the program aired, Wead served on his board of directors. Hinn's "church" still maintains its tax-exempt status—and its secrecy.

TBN continued to support Bush and the Republicans during Bush's first term. Conservative Republicans in TBN's headquarters state of California are frequently featured. Republican candidate Bill Simon was hosted by Matt and Laurie Crouch during the 2002 California gubernatorial primary campaign; Laurie sighed blissfully that "now we have somebody to vote for."[58] Congressman Dana Rohrabacher (R-CA) has been a guest, as has former congressman Randall "Duke" Cunningham, who appeared several years before he pleaded guilty to accepting bribes in exchange for defense contracts and was suspected of using Department of Homeland Security limousines to transport prostitutes to poker games. But at the time, Crouch, obviously pleased that his studio was graced with the presence of the powerful congressman and former Vietnam fighter pilot, exclaimed, "What a soul-winner he is! Every time he shares his powerful testimony, lives are touched, *and our SOULS TOTAL soars!* Thank God for precious men and women who love God are willing to serve and lead their country. Pray for them!"[59]

Just before the 2004 election, Crouch pulled out more ammunition in support of Bush. In one program in which Crouch expressed support for the war in Iraq, he griped about the "liberal left-wing media['s]" coverage of it. "In Jesus' name," he pleaded, clutching a Bible, "get out there and register to vote this November. I'm not telling you how to vote ... [but] check the voting records of those candidates you're voting on and see where they stand and how they line up with the holy word of God." Crouch then segued directly into praise for Bush for signing the ban on so-called partial-birth abortion, which Crouch described as an "evil doctor" sticking a needle into a baby's head as it is "hanging out" of the mother's birth canal.[60] Matt and Laurie Crouch later hosted Ann Coulter, whom they described as "a defender of patriotism" and "a defender of America." Promoting her book *How To Talk to A Liberal (If You Must)*, Coulter said that liberals are "anti-God," which is "why they hate George Bush so much." After the interview, the Crouches compared Coulter to Jesus.[61]

TBN continues to be an essential GOP campaign stop. In the
spring of 2007, John McCain made an appearance on TBN's "news
program," *Behind the Scenes*, hosted by Paul Crouch Jr. In a half-hour
softball interview in which Crouch repeatedly praised McCain, the
candidate pontificated on topics dear to the evangelical audience: his
faith, the "titanic" struggle between good and evil in the war on terror, and the vitality of Christian support for Israel.[62]

Copeland: The Most Important Religious Leader in the Nation

Crouch wasn't Wead's only ally in Bush's presidential campaign. After
Kenneth Copeland had proved his value during 1988 presidential
campaign, Wead recommended to George W. Bush that he pursue a
relationship with the televangelist. The adviser told Karl Rove in the
summer of 1998 that Copeland "is arguably one of the most important religious leaders in the nation." Wead recognized, however, that
Copeland, the leading figure in the Word of Faith movement, was
"doctrinally controversial," noting that the Assemblies of God re-
sented the money drain on its churches because of its members sending tithes and offerings to televangelists like Copeland. Nonetheless,
Wead described Copeland as a "gentleman . . . [who] will not use you
or exploit you. He is a very sincere, truly spiritual man, who can be a
friend and who will never stop praying for you."[63] Copeland, Wead
told both Bush and Rove, had been very helpful to Bush's father's
campaign in a "very discreet" way.

Discreet he is; unlike Parsley, Copeland never publicly touts his
relationship with Republican officials, nor does he give media interviews.[64] But Copeland reached out to Governor Bush, sending him,
through Wead, a copy of a book that claimed to prophesy events in
the West Bank based on the book of Ezekiel. Wead told the governor
that Copeland thought Bush "had to have the book" and considered
it "very urgent."[65] Copeland was present at a meeting Bush had with
evangelicals in Dallas, at which the group laid hands on the candi-

date and one pastor prayed for God to "put the mantle of a champion" on him.[66] Shortly before the election, Copeland called Wead to ask if the campaign had noticed that he mentioned Bush on his television program. Wead told Bush and Rove that "I assured him that it was having an impact."[67]

Copeland also asked Bush to help promote the political career of one of his black protégés, Keith Butler, whose Word of Faith church in Detroit has grown to twenty-two thousand members since its founding in 1979. Butler, who ran unsuccessfully for the Senate in 2006, has long-standing and deep roots with the GOP, and his career exemplifies the ways in which evangelicals successfully secured a place in the Republican Party apparatus in the 1980s. After changing his party affiliation in 1980, Butler became a GOP precinct chairman in 1984, and in 1989 he became the first Republican on the Detroit City Council since World War II. Also in 1989, Bush Sr. honored him at the White House after he was named one of ten "outstanding Americans" by the United States Junior Chamber of Commerce. In 1991 Bush invited him back to the White House to ask for political advice in the wake of the riots following the Rodney King police beatings. Butler was further rewarded with the deputy co-chair of the Republican National Convention and a seat on the GOP platform committee in 1992.[68]

Butler became an advocate for George W. Bush as well, joining with Michigan multimillionaire businessman and Bush Pioneer Heinz Prechter, who formed the group American Dreamers to raise money for Bush from minority donors. (Pioneers are those who raised at least $100,000 for Bush from other donors.) Prechter, who had raised over $1 million for Bush's father in 1988, became a kingmaker for then-governor Bush,[69] hosting a 1998 quail-hunting retreat with "twelve top GOP fundraisers at his 10,000-acre Texas ranch. Bush emerged from this hunt as the GOP moneyed elite's candidate," according to the watchdog group Public Citizen.[70] Butler met Bush at a gathering of religious leaders and businesspeople in

Austin in 1999 and said he was "moved by [Bush's] clear affirmation of faith" to support his candidacy.[71]

For his 2006 Senate run, which he lost in the primary, Butler received significant contributions from other Word of Faith pastors and their families, including Copeland, Hagee, Parsley, Hagin, and Mac Hammond, another Copeland protégé.[72] Hammond became the target of an IRS complaint in 2006 for endorsing Republican congressional candidate—and now representative—Michele Bachmann at his Living Word Church in Brooklyn Park, Minnesota, during an appearance at which Bachmann pronounced herself "a fool for Christ."[73] Hammond also put his name on a fund-raising letter endorsing Butler's candidacy.[74] Butler employed "one of the hottest Republican media firms," BrabenderCox, the same firm used by the Bush-Cheney reelection campaign, which Butler co-chaired in Michigan.[75]

Faith-Based Fraud

Butler was just one part of the Bush campaign's effort to reach out to black voters through Word of Faith churches. While Hagee was praising a potential faith-based initiative as the best alternative to Satan, Bush was busy currying favor with a group of black pastors who had been encouraged to join the faith-based initiative by then-representative J. C. Watts, the only black Republican in Congress. Harold Ray, a Florida pastor who is an Oral Roberts University graduate and former attorney, organized top black leaders, including Pearson, Long, Jakes, and Creflo Dollar (a Copeland protégé). Watts's staff worked with Ray, who in turn worked with the other megachurch pastors in building support for the faith-based initiative.

Once in office Bush used the faith-based initiative to woo evangelicals, and specifically the black prosperity preachers. The pastors were indulged with invitations to the White House, a dinner at the Library of Congress, and other events. "We were just like the rest of evangelical America," Carlton Pearson recalled. "Praise God, we got a man in office that's going to work for us, and support the church, and support fundamentalist Christian ideals and family values, and we were all very proud and thrilled. And then it just didn't pan out that way at all."[76]

During Bush's first term, the pastors "came to the White House fairly often," said Rev. Shelley Henderson, an African American GOP insider who worked on the faith-based legislation in Watts's office in the late 1990s. After Watts left office in 2003, Henderson received a political appointment in the Department of Education Office of Faith-Based Initiatives and then at the White House Office of Public Liaison, where she reported to Rove. Small groups of black pastors, including Jakes, Butler, Long, and Dollar, "sat right at the table with the President . . . and part of it, quite frankly, is it's an awesome place to be. When you get to come to the White House and be at the table with the President, I mean, that's major."[77] Long, who has led demonstrations against gay marriage, later played host to Bush and former presidents when Coretta Scott King's funeral was held at his church, where King's daughter is an associate pastor. In 2004 Long received a $1 million grant from the U.S. Administration on Children and Families under the faith-based initiative.[78]

Henderson, who embraces the prosperity gospel, said no one in the White House questioned bringing the heavy hitters of prosperity televangelism to the White House. She recognizes that "just like in anything else, there are those that are taking advantage," and that in some churches "the motivation is greed." But Henderson doesn't see that in the major players like Jakes, Dollar, Long, and Butler. In the White House, "no one asked me about it [the prosperity gospel]," she said. "To be frank, it's a numbers game. Numbers meaning, T. D. Jakes has 30,000 members. Not only does he have that, he has influence over millions of people on a weekly basis. . . . If he's on our team, then we can count on him using his influence to assist us, and it's all about the President getting elected and supported."[79]

The courting of the major black televangelists, while ostensibly to build support for the faith-based initiative, was done with an eye toward winning reelection in 2004, said Henderson. The number of black Republicans is not large, but GOP operatives consider it significant enough to turn an election, and reaching more black voters remains a vital GOP goal.[80] Bush did increase his standing among black voters in Ohio—a decisive state for electoral college votes in recent elections—from 9 percent in 2000 to 17 percent in 2004. Nationally, his share of the black vote increased only from 9 percent to 11 percent. That increased share of the black vote in 2004 was likely spurred by the gay marriage ban on Ohio's ballot that year, for which Parsley and Blackwell campaigned heavily.[81]

Henderson, whose job responsibility was to reach out to the black community, organized a First Ladies' Summit, to which she invited the wives of major black televangelists, including Serita Jakes and Deborah Butler, to a weekend affair. The wives have had intimate dinners with First Lady Laura Bush and met with the president, then-Republican National Committee (RNC) chair Ken Mehlman, Condoleezza Rice, and Virginia Thomas, the Supreme Court justice's wife. Henderson was able to sell the feting of the wives to Rove because "they are really the influential ones. . . . It was 2004 . . . the President was going up for reelection, and so we were really looking at how to get out in the faith community." Even though she left the White House in 2004, Henderson continues to host the summit annually on Martin Luther King weekend, and it always includes a visit to the White House.[82]

Copeland, Discreet; Parsley, Not So Much

Copeland continues to help the GOP in "discreet" ways. He has preached on "the responsibility of a righteous vote" and frequently hosts David Barton on his *Believer's Voice of Victory* program on topics such as "The Anointing to Rule" and "The Role of Christians in

Civil Government."[83] Barton is an Oral Roberts University graduate and the prolific president of WallBuilders, a nonprofit that disseminates Barton's reinterpretations of American history in service of the Texas GOP platform plank—written while Barton served as the state party vice chairman—that declares the United States a "Christian nation." Barton believes the separation of church and state is a "myth" and regularly brings pastors from across to the country to Capitol Hill for "exclusive briefing sessions with some of the top Christian Senators and Representatives now serving in Congress."[84] During the 2004 campaign, when he also appeared numerous times on Copeland's program, Barton was paid by the Republican National Committee to visit three hundred evangelical churches, where he advised pastors (incorrectly) that it is not illegal for them to endorse political candidates from the pulpit. In the waning weeks of the campaign, Barton admitted that the GOP kept the meetings "below the radar. . . . We work our tails off to stay out of the news."[85] Barton later joined forces with TBN to produce a television series to debunk what they consider to be the "myth" of the separation of church and state.[86]

Like Bush's 2000 campaign slogan, Compassionate Conservatism, Word of Faith preachers often give lip service to their church's community service projects yet worship at the altar of hyperindividualism and unregulated capitalism. As if a merely comfortable life were insufficient to demonstrate just how much God has blessed them, many of these televangelists spend millions of dollars of church funds on luxury jets, take huge salaries out of church coffers to build themselves mansions, and treat themselves to other luxuries like clothes, vacations, and high-end dinners. They use the free advertising of their churches and television shows to sell countless books, tapes, and DVDs of their sermons and sermonizing, raking in millions that go into for-profit church-related enterprises that line their own pockets. All of this activity is rationalized as obeying Jesus' command to spread the Gospel throughout the world. Yet it is all possible precisely because there is virtually no oversight of the preachers' activities. Tax-exempt churches do not file tax returns and are under no obligation to divulge their finances to donors or the public. Where profit-driven church meets the cornerstone of conservative economic ideology, televangelists have been enriching themselves in an unregulated marketplace trading on God, the cult of personality, and American dreams of riches and success.

Although some observers of the 2006 election have pronounced the conservative Christian movement dead, Parsley's preaching in the service at Huch's church reveals exactly why the Word of Faith movement will play a big role in keeping it alive through the 2008 elections and beyond. While Parsley's audience is under his spell, the mayhem is suddenly suspended when Parsley yells, "Stop! I just heard the Holy Ghost." The audience falls silent, hoping for a direct line from God. Instead, Parsley delivers a political speech.

Because he was the subject of a 2006 complaint to the Internal Revenue Service that he violated his church's tax-exempt status by repeatedly endorsing Blackwell's candidacy in the Ohio gubernatorial primary, Parsley treads carefully on partisan terrain. To his rapt audience, Parsley answers the question he says many people are asking him in the wake of the 2006 midterm election that was a disaster for Republicans, including Blackwell: "What happened to the values voters?" Parsley insists that they didn't go away; they just became what he calls "integrity voters," meaning that "they stood up and said regardless of what you espouse with your rhetoric, if your lifestyle doesn't produce godliness, you're not going to have our vote."

Parsley takes his self-created opportunity to parlay his own rendering of "integrity" into his speech, melding his prosperity gospel with a message of individualistic entitlement that fuels the Word of Faith movement. Parsley's own wealth is built on the tithes and offerings he solicits through his church, television show, and Web site, but he justifies taking the donations by claiming that he serves God's kingdom by giving some of the money away. He says that "the government cannot do what the church must," insisting that the church must focus on issues of justice in addition to those of "righteousness." He claims that "if every church in Ohio had done what mine has done in the last year, there would not be one hungry person in the state. Not one hungry person." But he doesn't say what it is his church has done; did it take in the homeless or help people find jobs? That is not clear. But the Word of Faith message, the gospel of money and greed is clear, and Parsley implies—though he offers no proof—that his wealth is godly because he redistributes it. "It's time we stop being intimidated by the naysayers who say it's godly to have nothing. That's a lie, that's a lie. It's godly to believe for more than enough because there are always those who don't have enough."[87]

He will not document his generosity, however. Parsley operates his ministry under tight familial control, with a complete lack of transparency and accountability. But mixed up in his contrived message of his own generosity, he implores his audience to be generous to *him*. That, the Word of Faith credo goes, will result in givers being blessed with their own financial harvest. With the thousands in the audience repeating each phrase, he tells them to "throw your hands up and say, 'Bless me, Lord! I'm a giver. I'm a tither. I'm going to bless your kingdom. And I receive financial abundance!'"

TWO

Health, Wealth, and Purpose

> I remember when we needed a van for the ministry
> to carry our equipment. My daughter Kellie came to
> me and said, "Daddy, I want to be the first to give
> money for this truck." She had a couple of dollars,
> so she gave it, and we made an agreement together.
> Then she started confessing the return on her
> money and got it! It didn't take her several months,
> and she didn't start whining about it—she simply
> said, "In the Name of Jesus, it's mine!"
> —KENNETH COPELAND, *The Laws of Prosperity*

On a brisk March Sunday morning at Rhema Bible Church in Broken Arrow, Oklahoma, Kenneth Hagin has just finished reading the church announcements. Having dispensed with statistics about how many people the street evangelism team has saved, how the church school basketball team is doing, and urgings that his congregants attend an upcoming seminar on entrepreneurship ("so you can funnel finances into this ministry. That's as much the call of God as preaching behind this pulpit"), he faces his congregation with a clarion call.

"What time is it?" he bellows.

"Investment time!" is the obedient reply of several thousand congregants, who all pull out wallets and checkbooks to stuff the offering envelopes made available on the back of every pew. As they turn over their money, they recite the offering prayer:

39

This is my seed. I sow it into the Kingdom of God. I sow
because I love God and I want to see RHEMA Bible Church
continue to fulfill what God has called us to do.

I believe that as I sow my seed, it shall be given unto me—
good measure, pressed down, shaken together, and running
over! It shall come back to me in many ways!

I thank you, Lord, for good opportunities coming my way. I
thank You that the windows of Heaven are opening because of
my obedience to sow my seed.

I thank You, Lord, for the favor of God upon my life and the
grace to prosper, as You have promised me in Your Word.

Here at Rhema is where you can see Word of Faith teaching in its
purest form. (The translation of the Greek word *rhema* is roughly
"spoken word," or in Christian parlance, the word God speaks to his
children.) Hagin's father, the evangelist and faith healer Kenneth
Hagin Sr., known around Rhema as "Brother Hagin," is credited with
founding the modern faith movement in the 1950s and spreading its
message beyond the reach of his tent revivals when he created the
Rhema Bible Training Center.[1] The center has produced an army of
twenty-six thousand graduates, about two thousand of whom, including 2006 GOP Senate candidate Keith Butler, pastor their own
churches. Brother Hagin, who died in 2003, laid the groundwork;
now most of the major Word of Faith churches have a Bible college
and a ministerial fellowship, through which graduates replicate the
church under the umbrella of the mentor's ministry. Dan McConnell,
a scholar of the charismatic movement, has compared Hagin's meteoric celebrity in the 1960s to "some sort of overnight adolescent
craze. . . . With the exception of the media giants, the prime time televangelists such as Oral Roberts, Pat Robertson, and Jim Bakker, it
would be difficult to name a circuit ministry that grew faster in the
late 1970s than that of Kenneth Hagin."[2]

It is from the elder Hagin that the movement derives its principles, which are replicated in various combinations by countless evangelists and their imitators, including Parsley, Hagee, Hinn, Copeland, Long, and Jakes. They have all both influenced and been influenced by the expression of Word of Faith and adapted it to their churches and television ministries for maximum profit. Brother Hagin was revolutionary, says one of his protégés, Karen Jensen, because he taught "the authority of the believer. There's things that God wants you to have and has given you as rights and privileges in Christ Jesus." She cited Luke 10:19, adding, "in Jesus, we have this authority and we use it by our faith. By faith, Moses did what he did, in Hebrews 11. Brother Hagin really had a revelation on that that nobody had. I mean, it's the same faith. But nobody had preached it like that."[3] Hagin claimed to have been visited by Jesus, "an experience that seems to be a virtual requirement for a Word-Faith televangelist," who then imparted this new doctrine to him directly.[4]

Word of Faith: Christianity or Heresy?

In the last quarter of the twentieth century, Word of Faith chagrined many Christians, including charismatics. The modern charismatic or neo-Pentecostal movement traces its roots to the 1906 Azusa Street Revival in Los Angeles, at which a group of people, mostly black and poor, were "filled with the Holy Spirit" and spoke in tongues as evidence of it. The term *Pentecostal* is from the Greek word *Pentecost*, meaning the "fiftieth day" after Christ's ascension (corresponding to the Jewish holiday of Shavuot), during which, according to the New Testament book of Acts, the first followers of Christ are said to have spoken in other tongues when they received the Holy Spirit. Modern-day charismatics see Azusa Street as the popular beginning of a twentieth-century renewal that became "'the most phenomenal event of twentieth century

Christianity.'"[5] But the assimilation of Word of Faith teaching into the charismatic movement has caused rifts.

McConnell, a critic, has shown that Hagin plagiarized the teaching of early-twentieth-century radio evangelist E. W. Kenyon, whose writings can still be found for sale in the bookstores of Word of Faith churches. Hagin's plagiarism, McConnell contends, is evidence that Word of Faith is not rooted in Pentecostalism but rather in the late-nineteenth-century "mind science" or "New Thought" movement—which emphasized the power of positive thinking—and which critics say is "clearly heretical."[6] Hank Hanegraaff, who hosts the *Bible Answer Man* program on the conservative Christian Salem Radio Network, is a leading charismatic detractor of the Word of Faith movement from a conservative biblical perspective. Hanegraaff describes Word of Faith as "cultic" because it is rooted in metaphysics rather than sound biblical teaching. The Word of Faith movement, Hanegraaff says, "was spawned by the unholy marriage of 19th century New Thought metaphysics with the flamboyance and abuses of post–World War II revivalism. It should therefore come as no surprise that its doctrine and practices are palpably unbiblical."[7] He has called the Word of Faith movement the "greatest threat to [evangelical Christianity] from within."[8]

Ole Anthony, president of the Trinity Foundation in Dallas, challenges the Word of Faith preachers with more than just his Bible. Anthony started one of the nation's first religious television stations in Dallas in the early 1970s. But he soon became disenchanted with religious broadcasting, particularly how it is bought and sold. Trinity, which takes in homeless people to its small community of houses in east Dallas, has a team of licensed private investigators who have helped major news outlets expose some of the most notorious examples of televangelism fraud, including Tilton and Hinn. "I'm a charismatic, in terms of speaking in tongues and believing," says Anthony. Referring to the prosperity televangelists, he added, "I call them charismaniacs."[9]

Scriptural Challenges

Hanegraaff takes issue with the Word of Faith interpretation of Hebrews 11 that forms the basis for Hagin's and Copeland's teachings. The Word of Faith teachers maintain that God spoke the world into existence, and as a "little god," a person's "force of faith is released by words" through which they can call things into existence for themselves.[10] But using translations of Hebrews 11 from the original Greek, Hanegraaff counters that faith does not give human beings authority over their material world. "Far from being some tangible material, faith is a *channel of living trust*—an *assurance*—which stretches from man to God. . . . Far from meaning 'tangible stuff,' it specifically refers to the assurance that God's promises never fail, even if sometimes we do not experience their fulfillment in our mortal existence."[11]

Although the charismatic critics of Word of Faith also believe, as Hanegraaff puts it, "in divine healing and in God's provision for every detail of our lives," they reject the Word of Faith credo that those with faith are entitled to health and wealth.[12] Word of Faith proponents start with God's covenant with Abraham in Genesis and find dozens of other uses of the word *prosper* in both the Old and New Testaments to support their claims. In the Gospel of John, for example, they point to the verse "Beloved, I wish above all things that thou mayest prosper and be in health, even as thy soul prospereth" to claim that God wants believers to be rich.[13] Using hermeneutics, Hanegraaff and others have shown that John's message was a standard greeting in antiquity and that the Greek word translated as *prosper* merely meant he hoped things would go well. It had nothing to do with money.[14]

In the Sermon on the Mount, Jesus taught that God knows what you need before you ask for it. But the prosperity preachers, McConnell charges, have distorted the word *need* to mean something beyond "necessity" and have failed to make "any distinction be-

tween a *need* and a *want*, and a *want* and a *lust*" for items such as
new houses, fancy cars, and fine clothing.[15] The fixation on wealth,
McConnell argues, is "a carnal accommodation to the crass materialism of American culture." It serves not only to "rationalize the dis-
parity between rich and poor. It actually degrades the poor, claiming
that their poverty is a result of 'dishonoring' God."[16]

In the African American church, the disregard—and even denigration—of the poor among Word of Faith preachers has produced a
wave of criticism. At a 2005 meeting of the Samuel DeWitt Proctor
Conference, a group of black preachers who meet regularly to discuss the state of the black church, critics included Jeremiah Wright,
pastor to Obama's church, Chicago's Trinity United Church of
Christ. Wright, who preaches black liberation theology, charged that
black prosperity megachurches were not addressing hunger, poverty,
or other social issues.[17] (After Obama launched his presidential campaign, Wright was disparaged by conservative commentators, including Sean Hannity, who falsely accused him of being a black separatist.[18]) Liberation theology, which teaches followers to confront
and change unjust institutions, is more in line with a Martin Luther
King Jr. model of the black church than the individualistic prosperity church. Emory University theologian Robert M. Franklin calls the
prosperity gospel "the single greatest threat to the historical legacy
and core values of the contemporary black church tradition."[19]

Despite its critics, because Word of Faith employs (or possibly co-
opts) many of the features of the twentieth-century charismatic
movement, it has become inextricably linked to that movement.
Although many present-day Word of Faith preachers started out in
Pentecostal denominations—many of the white evangelists in the
Assemblies of God, and many black ones in the Church of God in
Christ—the modern charismatic movement is increasingly nondenominational. Many of its adherents left denominational churches to
establish or attend what are known as independent charismatic
churches. In contrast to traditional Pentecostalism, which shuns

worldly materialism and secular culture, the neo-Pentecostal move-ment has embraced the trappings of modern consumerist life. Yet it views every transaction in the context of "spiritual warfare" between the world of Satan and the world of God. And every challenge is a threat: after Hanegraaff met with TBN head Paul Crouch in the early 1990s, Crouch "looked into the lens of the television camera and an-grily declared, 'If you want to criticize Ken Copeland for his preach-ing on faith, or Dad [Brother] Hagin, get out of my life! I don't even want to talk to you or hear you. I don't want to see your ugly face. Get out of my face, in Jesus' name.'"[20]

Word of Faith has left an indelible mark on the charismatic move-ment in the second half of the century, melding fundamentalist reli-gion with a contemporary capitalist enterprise in which the free mar-ket reigns and government regulation or intervention is seen as Satanic. Word of Faith thrives in twenty-first-century American life, where religious fundamentalism meets a culture of celebrity, where people hold out hope for their own prosperity despite abundant ev-idence of a winner-take-all economy, and where individualistic capi-talism becomes even more potent when it is believed to be sanc-tioned by God.

Jesus Was a Wealthy Man

On the March Sunday I attend Rhema Bible Church, Hagin, as if for my benefit, is preaching on the basics of Word of Faith, found in Mark 11:22–24. His father, born premature and sickly into a dys-functional rural Texas family in 1917, claimed to have been saved by Mark 11:23 while on his deathbed as a teenager. Hagin points to that verse ("Whatever things you ask when you pray . . . you will re-ceive them."), which became the hallmark of his father's Word of Faith teaching. As his father explained the scriptural authority for positive confession, "believe in your heart, say it with your mouth, and 'he shall have whatsoever he saith.'"[21] Like most Word of Faith teaching, the interpretation of biblical verses is devoid of metaphor; like Jesus' pronouncement that faith and prayer could move a mountain, Word of Faith proponents would probably actually try to move a mountain if they thought it was physically possible.

According to Word of Faith critics, Hagin's discussion of the power of faith, based on Mark 11, is flawed. When Hagin tells his followers to have "the God kind of faith," he is misinterpreting Mark. Robert M. Bowman, author of *The Word-Faith Controversy*, writes that the verse refers to "the kind of faith that has God as its object," not "the kind of faith God has."[22] Jesus was not, according to McConnell, "conferring godhead upon men who have faith." Rather, Jesus was urging his followers to have faith in God's "saving deeds."[23]

The highly individualistic nature of Word of Faith is on full display in Hagin's preaching on Mark 11. Quoting his father, Hagin advises his congregants to "get your own faith because no one is as interested in you as you are." In an odd turn for anyone who would expect a pastor to be fully absorbed with caring for his flock, Hagin admits that "people ask me to pray for them, but I don't think about them all the time." He asks the audience if people ask them to pray for them, and audience members nod and murmur assent. Hagin gets them to agree with him that nonetheless they don't think about these people all the time.

But, Hagin goes on, "People think about themselves every day. . . . What am I going to wear?" he asks, mimicking a hypothetical ordinary Joe, thinking about himself. "That's easy," he continues, "I got three shirts, three pairs of pants, I wear that shirt with that pair of pants, and then the next day the other . . . and then I turn around and start over." Then, reverting to himself, Hagin boasts, "I've been there, done that, but now, praise God, through my faith, I got more than three shirts and three pairs of pants." His kind of faith, he says, is "the kind of faith that speaks and has." The Bible "tells you how to speak and how to get something going on." Hagin concedes that his flock is going to face obstacles. But "you're going to have to speak down those obstacles.... You've got to ... tell sickness to leave, ... command resources to come."

The way to achieve your goals, Hagin says, is to "act like you have it.... Rejoice! Declare, 'I have it, it's mine!'" He encourages the audience to "keep saying it til you see it." Three times a day, Hagin says, one should thank God for one's finances. But he's not just interested in his followers' prosperity. "I thank God every day that God will bring finances to you, members of Rhema Bible Church ... because I want you to have finances, but second, I want you to give money to Rhema Bible Church."

"How many of you have come up the ladder since coming to this [church]?" He asks. People cheer and wave their hands in the air. He tells them, "Don't be satisfied because God wants us to climb the ladder.... Speak the word," he tells them. "If you want to sell something, go over to it and say, 'I declare you *sold* in the name of Jesus!'" If you want something, he continues, "keep calling it into existence and thank God for it."

At Rhema I am sitting next to a couple, Angie and Mike West, she a hairdresser and he a former factory worker, who are first-year students at the Bible Training Center. The Wests were living in Michigan when, Angie says, God told her to go to Rhema and study at the Bible Training Center. Mirroring the Word of Faith expression of her mentors, she speaks of a personal conversation with God, who placed his will within her body. He "stirred in my heart that whole year, about change, something different, and yet I was real comfortable where we were.... And I was doing laundry, and I felt the Lord dropped in my heart, go to Rhema. And I said, no. And he said, you said you would go and do whatever ... and he said, go to Rhema. And I said, OK. So I said, Mike, let's just go to Rhema." So the Wests sold their house, packed up their lives, and moved to Broken Arrow. Since being at Rhema, Angie feels that "we can have whatsoever we ask for, according to his word. We're not going to go out there and get stupid, OK? But we can have whatsoever we ask, according to the word of God. And if you know the word of God, then you'll know what to ask for."

On financial matters, the Wests believe that no one would want to be a Christian if Christians were poor, so it must be God's will that Christians be rich. As Angie puts it, "If a Christian is a poor, desperate-type person, who would want to be a Christian? Does God want us to be poor, desolate people? Christ himself did not come on this earth and be poor and desolate. He was a wealthy man." Mike added that "if you look at the history of the Bible and look at the Jews, and how they weren't poor throughout their history. When they were serving God with their whole heart, they were on top of the world financially, too. . . . They were prosperous people, and they were healthy."[24]

But Christians shouldn't expect money to fall out of heaven just because they're believers, Angie insists. "We've got to do our part. We go to work every day, we work hard, we do what's right according to the word, we don't steal time from our boss, and we're blessed. That matters. God honors the faithful." Because of that, she doesn't feel as though Christians should help just anyone. "Sometimes, it's like—somebody, you know they have a need, but they're not doing their part as far as doing what they can to help themselves. I don't believe God is going to put it on our hearts to go and meet their need. Because they've got to have that faith that Hagin talked about, and say, you know, I'm doing what God's called me to do, therefore I believe, that I know, because I'm doing my part, God's going to bless and honor that."

Since Hagin founded his Bible Training Center in 1974, there has been, according to McConnell, an "ever-widening circle of Hagin imitators—and imitators of the imitators *ad infinitum*—who have turned the Faith movement into a multimillion dollar enterprise. . . . [and who have] propagated Hagin's gospel in a manner analogous to spontaneous combustion."[25] Copeland, who probably makes more money than any of the other televangelists, most closely replicates

Hagin's teaching, and Copeland's own many protégés now replicate his. Copeland is a sort of heir apparent to Hagin, and televangelists like Hagee and Parsley collaborate with him:[26] preaching prosperity, lobbying for Armageddon, and affirming the supposed "Christian heritage" of America.[27] The replication continues today as many of the more successful evangelists insinuate themselves into politics, launch new churches, and send out graduates of their Bible colleges to preach prosperity.

Although he carries his father's torch, Hagin is hardly the movement's most magnetic spokesperson or its greatest celebrity. In contrast to the staged hipness of many of his younger competitors, Hagin possesses a rather lackluster presence. While the sugary pop music of the praise and worship team warms up the congregation before the service, Hagin and his wife, Lynette, look a bit like parents chaperoning a high school dance, bemusedly standing off to the side, uncertain as to how to react to the music. In photographs he often has a deer-in-the-headlights look. But because he carries the mantle of his father, today's leading Word of Faith moguls owe their empires—and their personal wealth—to him.

Sow a Seed, Reap a Harvest

While Hagin provided the fundamental principles of Word of Faith, just a few miles away, Oral Roberts contributed his part. Roberts, a self-made faith healer who founded his eponymous university in 1963 and was the first prime-time televangelist, is credited with the seed-faith principle that underlies most Word of Faith fund-raising. Roberts notoriously claimed on television in January 1987 that God told him he would "call him home" if he did not raise $8 million by the end of March; he raised $9.1 million.[28]

The seed-faith principle provides that if you sow a seed (i.e., give a tithe or offering to your church, your pastor, or a televangelist), you will reap a hundredfold, or even a thousandfold, harvest. In other

words, if you give your pastor your money, you will receive a supernatural return on your investment. According to Hanegraaff, planting
a seed "is virtually synonymous with 'mail me money.' The seed-faith
gimmick is little more than a give-to-get gospel of greed."[29] The
Word of Faith preachers twist Scripture, Hanegraaff contends, "even
trying to use Galatians 6:7 . . . ('whatsoever a man soweth, that shall
he also reap') to make [their] point."[30]

As Copeland describes it, "In tithing, you are laying the foundation for financial success and abundance. You are establishing de-
posits with God that can be used when you need them."[31] Copeland
rejects the worldly financial system as "complex and very poor in operation" while God's financial system functions perfectly—at least for
him. The problem with the world's financial system, says Copeland,
"is that there is a spiritual mad dog loose in it and his name is Satan."
He tells his followers not to invest in the worldly financial system
and not to borrow from a bank. If you *believe* and *confess* according
to his principles, "when you stand on the covenant of God and exer-
cise your rights as a tither, Satan has no chance against you. God will
rebuke the devourer for your sake."[32]

Even if you're not financially able to begin tithing, Copeland insists that "you cannot afford to wait! The tithe belongs to God in the
first place." Here he cites the favorite verses of the tithe mongers,
Malachi 3:8–9: "Will a man rob God? Yet ye have robbed me. But ye
say, Wherein have we robbed thee? In tithes and offerings. Ye are
cursed with a curse: for ye have robbed me." Conveniently for
Copeland, he profits as he implores his followers to "start tithing
now! If you don't have any money, find something you do have and
give it today. There is no faster or surer way to break that curse."[33]

Roberts has recognized Copeland as the embodiment of a
merger between his and Hagin's ministries. "Brother Hagin had a
tremendous influence on [the Copelands]," Roberts wrote recently.
"And so they had a merging of my ministry, of the healing ministry,
of the seed-faith ministry that I had introduced to the world; and

Brother Hagin's fantastic ministry on faith and the Word of God."[34] If Copeland represents a merger, Hagee, Parsley, and other imitators are his subsidiaries. Parsley has written that "the Bible says that to withhold the tithe is to rob God" and that people who don't tithe "want to blame God, blame the economy, blame the government, blame their job and blame their boss." But, says Parsley, God places the blame "right between your nose and your chin"—meaning, once again, that the failure to believe and confess the word is the cause of all your problems.[35] The external world "is rooted in greed," but in "God's kingdom, if you sow a seed, you will reap. . . . Sowing is the key that unlocks the kingdom of heaven."[36] Again, Satanic forces are at work in the world's financial system, but God's financial system works supernaturally to open up the gates of heaven. To his congregation, the tithe is divinely required: "If you want to be obedient to God, I want you to take out a seed right now."[37]

Hagee makes clear that people who engage in revelation thinking are controlled by God, not by their minds, and therefore will have more financial abundance in their lives: "Reason givers are controlled by their minds. They do not ask God how much they should give; they ask their CPA. Revelation givers are controlled by the Holy Spirit. They see God as their supplier. Revelation givers do not give according to what they have, but according to what God can supply."[38] For critics of Word of Faith, revelation knowledge is unbiblical, because "*the Bible itself denies that a perfect knowledge of God is attainable in this life.* The perfect knowledge of God—and of man, for that matter—will not be attainable until 'the Perfect One' returns. This was clearly the teaching of Paul."[39] Revelation knowledge creates "delusions of grandeur," as "the Faith 'supermen' become 'kings in life' and 'the bondage breakers for the rest of the human race.' Nowhere does the Bible teach that certain believers could attain to the status of a savior or redeemer." McConnell calls this lack of humility, so different from the Apostle Paul, an example of "the messiah-complex that permeates much of the charismatic movement."[40]

But that absence of humility results in the belief in one's power to call things into existence, including prosperity, with the force of one's words.

Hagee writes that "you will never prosper until you believe and confess that it is God's will for you to prosper." Like Copeland, he believes that there are two economic forces at work, those of God and those of Satan, and "you do not qualify for God's abundance until you become God's child." And exhibiting the antiworldly, antigovernment position of Word of Faith, Hagee maintains that "God Almighty controls the economy of America, and God controls your income! Your source is God, not the United States government. . . . When you give to God, He controls your income. There is no such thing as fixed income in the Kingdom of God. Your income is controlled by your giving." Believing or not believing in these principles is one's choice, and if you make the wrong choice, you've clearly sided with Satan and will be cursed financially: "The difference between living a life of prosperity and a life of poverty is a matter of choice. . . . Tithing is a choice. If you choose to not tithe, you will be living under a financial curse."[41]

Similarly, Hinn maintains that "true biblical prosperity is not an accident—it is a decision!" Like many of the televangelists, Hinn loves to describe how he got so rich by believing in these principles: "I discovered long ago that God's laws concerning giving and receiving are fixed and immutable laws that no man and no circumstance can change. The Lord has promised that when we sow seed in faith we will reap a harvest. This is an unfailing, eternal promise that cannot be broken. . . . It is because of sowing in faith that God will place seed in the hands of the sower. And because of that the Lord will multiply the seed of the sower."[42] Hinn's favorite tactic is the canard that the world is ending soon, and he needs as much money as possible so he can travel as much as possible and save as many souls as possible before the end. "Truly we are running out of time, for the Lord declared in His Word that He will do a quick work in the last days!" he wrote in an e-mail to supporters, echoing the sort of plea he makes on practically a daily basis on his television show, *This Is Your Day!* "I have seen God pour out His financial blessings, time after time, upon our precious partners who have stood with me in the past. I know it will happen, even more, during the coming glorious days."[43]

Golden Child of a New Generation

As Hagin and Roberts aged, a fresh face—himself a Roberts protégé—took up the mantle of promoting the careers of the next generation of charismatic preachers. That fresh face was Carlton Pearson, an effervescent, talented Oral Roberts University (ORU) graduate, so close to Roberts that the televangelist referred to him as "my black son." Pearson, who had grown up in the Church of God in Christ, the largest black Pentecostal denomination, came to ORU to attend college and was handpicked by Roberts to be part of his elite World Action Singers, which appeared on national television and traveled the globe with the televangelist. Catapulted into the spotlight by both his magnetism and the esteem in which Roberts held him, in 1981 he began pastoring a successful megachurch in Tulsa, Higher Dimensions. Throughout the decade, Pearson had his own television program and appeared on TBN, Pat Robertson's *700 Club*, and on Jim and Tammy Faye Bakker's *PTL Club*. He was, in Shayne Lee's words, a "golden child."

In 1988 Pearson began hosting an annual Azusa Conference—named for the early-twentieth-century Pentecostal revival—which each year drew tens of thousands of people to Tulsa to see the new talent of the prosperity movement. Pearson was not just Roberts's golden child, he was the movement's. He served on ORU's board, maintaining close relationships with Word of Faith giants Copeland and Hinn and acting as a talent agent of sorts for others' careers. Many of today's superstars—including Parsley, Jakes, and Joyce

Meyer—owe part of their phenomenal success to appearing at Azusa, a rite of passage for anyone who wanted to make it big in the charismatic world.

Probably Pearson's most successful career launch was Jakes, who capitalized on that opportunity to transform himself from a poor country preacher from West Virginia—a narrative he still emphasizes—into the success he is today, with his thirty-five-thousand-member Potters House Church in Dallas, numerous best-selling books, sizable speaking fees, and the attention of presidents and presidential hopefuls. Pearson believes that his old friend, now "an American icon," would have achieved the same fame and notoriety with or without Azusa, because "that's part of his destiny.... He didn't plan to be a small-time operator the rest of his life. He saw Azusa, he admired what it was and would like to do the same thing. It wasn't just about him preaching. He wanted to present ministry grandiose like that."[44] Jakes's career skyrocketed after Pearson arranged for TBN's Paul Crouch to hear a seven-minute clip of his preaching at Azusa, after which the TV mogul helped Jakes land his own show.

As Jakes has evolved, his style of preaching has focused more on an uplifting, I-feel-your-pain, Oprah-esque approach. Compared to other prosperity preachers, Jakes emphasizes personal empowerment rather than personal wealth (although wealth, to be sure, is desirable but not a goal in and of itself). He frequently parlays a more accepted interpretation of Scripture into his self-empowerment message, such as when he preached on how God used Moses despite his weakness (stuttering, an impediment that Jakes himself overcame) instead of his more eloquent brother Aaron to receive the Ten Commandments.[45] Subject to criticism for his luxurious lifestyle, even when he was in West Virginia, he now lives lavishly in Texas, with his mansion, private plane, custom-made suits, and a Bentley. When he baptized football stars Deion Sanders and Emmitt Smith, he sent out a press release.

Jakes deliberately uses a self-empowerment message to appeal to people's longing for self-improvement, not just spiritually but financially as well. "We live in this consumerist age where people want to be rich," said Shayne Lee. "On the one hand, it's very American where the underdog makes it, the Rocky Balboa story. On the other hand, now he's on the side of success, and he can empower you to join him because the ultimate goal as a contemporary American is to be rich and to consume all the things you want." But Jakes's message creates false hope, said Lee, since there's little or no chance that anyone hearing his sermon on a Sunday morning will end up like him, a fact that to Lee is "one of the more upsetting aspects of a popular branch of neo-Pentecostalism. . . . This idea that you're pointing at of God wants you to be rich, God wants you to succeed, all you need to do is apply these principles, that's popular and that's what a lot of these preachers are preaching and I do think it brings a false sense of hope because I don't think it's a universal gospel. It's an American gospel."[46]

"A Business Decision to Stay Away from Carlton Pearson"

Today, Pearson is an emblem of how neo-Pentecostalism is deeply threatened by challenges to its religious fundamentalism. After years of evolving toward the view, in 2005 Pearson publicly rejected the notion of hell. For this apostasy, for preaching what he calls the "gospel of inclusion," the golden child was roundly denounced by his old friends, even Jakes. "How can God say, mercy endures forever, supposedly, and he hates forever. He'd have to hate people to torture them forever; that's absurd and vulgar," Pearson told me. "But that doesn't sit well at all with the Rod Parsleys and the T. D. Jakeses and anybody else. I mean, none of those guys embrace my message." In that dichotomous world of Pentecostalism, says Pearson, "the only hell is the one we create here," as people follow "angry and unforgiving and intolerant and

very judgmental" preachers. Christianity itself, he adds, "has become the Antichrist. Because *anti* doesn't mean against it, it means
'besides.' Our religion has become a cult following of Jesus. And it's
scary to see what we've deteriorated into." [47]

Cast off by his old friends, Pearson now seems to look back on
the days of Azusa with a combination of nostalgia and regret. And
the regret has to do with money. "Once you walk across that platform [at the Azusa Conference], you could get enough invitations for
the next year to earn an additional quarter of a million dollars. . . .
[Others would] invite that same speaker to their conference, and it's
almost as if my stamp of approval, or Azusa's stamp of approval, was
on that conference." On top of honoraria, "most of these guys were
prominent enough to raise big offerings. . . . That's what kind of
caused me to back away—it became very, very financially motivated."
Pearson added that "I was beginning to feel like a pet for preachers.
That I was prostituting the virtue of the conference to people who
just saw it as a stepping stone for their own prominence."[48]

Pearson played a significant role in bringing together black and
white preachers and audiences, a fact that Parsley took particular
note of. "He [Parsley] started inviting the same speakers that we had
at Azusa, African American speakers and so that enhanced—it did
not necessarily enhance *him*, it enhanced his conference," said
Pearson. "I'm not saying that was his motive," Pearson continued,
"but Rod saw our style—I remember he said one time, 'Carlton
Pearson is not the only one who can dance.' And he started dancing
on the platform. And he really couldn't dance. He looked like a
white man having a seizure." Now, Pearson believes, "Parsley is staying alive in a ministry by appealing to the paranoia of the funda-
mentalists in America, . . . using this alarmist tactic to get funding. . . .
He's appealing to their fears and their paranoias about the end of the
world, about Muslims taking over, about gays taking over, about the
immoralists taking over, and if he did not do that, I think his money
would dry up." For most of the preachers who have shunned him,

"it's not a theological issue, it's a business decision, to stay away from Carlton Pearson."[49]

Pearson, who grew up poor in San Diego, doesn't "think every prosperity preacher is wrong. I just feel like that general spirit is . . . beginning to form malignancies within our [charismatics'] expression." Pearson rejects the accusation that parishioners gave their last pennies to their preacher in response to the command to "sow a seed," but he did acknowledge that many people did give consistently, and when they fell on hard times, they did not get any assistance from their church. "I don't think that in general, some of these big ministries would help individuals like they should." But on the other hand, Pearson doesn't apologize for the wealth of someone like Jakes, because "he sells million-dollar books" and is entitled to his millions. "What concerns me," says Pearson, "is if money is motive. It can be part of the blessing, the harvest. But if you are commercializing and merchandizing the ministry in a way that your nonprofit organization becomes your profit, in a grandiose way, then I think that that's where we have some issues." Yet Pearson clearly celebrates the success of African American preachers. "We don't make vows to poverty, you can't preach poor people into wealth and be poor. So it's just a different day when the poor, humble, beaten-down preacher waited for somebody to bring him a chicken dinner to survive; that was a hundred years ago. That will never happen again."[50]

Jakes's meteoric success, says Pearson, is a point of pride for black neo-Pentecostals, who used to be ashamed of their charismatic religious expression, such as speaking in tongues, and are now thrilled to have a celebrity preacher who makes that expression culturally acceptable:

> So when he [Jakes] gets on television, he has eighty thousand
> in a stadium and they're all jumping and screaming and shout-
> ing and doing things that we did almost embarrassingly fifty
> years ago; that's one of the things I was doing with Azusa. I
> wanted to make Pentecost pretty. I wanted to make that

expression eloquent and elegant and acceptable and vogue. . . . Because we [black Pentecostals] were nobodies fifty years ago. We lived in little ghetto churches, in storefronts. We had backwards preachers who could barely read, and most of our founders—the founder of my denomination had a second grade education. . . . My great grandfather was a preacher, could barely read. My dad could barely read . . . and so we're still saying 'wow, you mean you're packing out stadiums? And using hotel ballrooms, and packing out hotels and every room in hotels we weren't even allowed to live in just thirty years ago, forty years ago? . . . Suddenly, the black preacher is *somebody.*[51]

Today, Jakes has become what Pearson was: the broker with the power to make or break others' careers, or at least enhance them by giving them an appearance at a well-attended conference. Jakes helped launch the career of evangelist Paula White, who is emerging as "the Oprah of the evangelical world now." White is a slender blonde woman who represents "a kind of trendy, sporty, pretty model" of the evangelist, according to Lee, who has also studied the trajectory of her career. White has personally pastored Donald Trump and Michael Jackson and appears regularly on Tyra Banks's show to provide "life skills" consulting and is extremely popular with African American audiences.[52] She was among a small group of high-powered evangelical leaders invited to meet Mitt Romney at his home as he attempted to allay evangelical concerns about his Mormon faith before launching his presidential campaign.[53]

Over his career Jakes has continually reinvented himself, moving away from the more traditional Pentecostal style of preaching about the Holy Ghost and the devil, and even moving away from prosperity preaching to a self-empowerment message. His latest best seller, *Reposition Yourself: Living Life without Limits,* merges that self-help, self-empowerment message with the consumerist religion with which Jakes is now associated. "Jakes is just as much a shrewd businessman as he is a preacher," said Lee. Jakes has become a "powerful person," Lee added, particularly in the black community, with influence over whether magazines like *Ebony* and *Charisma* review a book that may contain less than glowing portrayals of him.[54] As a de facto leader and spokesman, then, Jakes has the power and influence to address abuses within the charismatic movement by preachers and televangelists, particularly with regard to the authoritarianism and the spiritual control they maintain over their congregants. Instead, at best, he remains silent. At worst, he ratifies the abuses.

Spiritual Alignment and Kingdom Order

One person whose teaching Jakes has ratified is Mark Hanby, whose career received a boost after he appeared at the same Azusa Conference as Jakes. Virtually unknown outside charismatic circles, Hanby is an extremely influential teacher to pastors, and many have followed and adapted his teaching on "spiritual alignment" and "kingdom order"—in other words, how to structure the church to maximize the protection of the preacher. Disgraced televangelist Jimmy Swaggart called on him for counseling in the 1980s, and through the 1990s, said Lee, "he was always there by Pearson's side or was always there as a kind of cherished leader in the movement."[55] Pearson said that pastors who have connected with Hanby and view him as a teacher and spiritual father are "all over the country. Almost everywhere he goes."[56] Eddie Long, a protégé of Hanby's, once took his mentor along on a White House visit during Clinton's presidency, and Clinton recognized Hanby from the Arkansas preaching circuit.[57]

Hanby has credited accused sexual abuser Earl Paulk as his "spiritual father." Others who are prominent on TBN and have been influenced by Hanby include Myles Munroe, a favorite on the Word of Faith circuit who teaches on "kingdom principles" (which he once explained on TBN as being not about democracy but about authority), and Tommy Tenney, who has collaborated on TBN-produced films. After Hanby and Jakes met at Azusa in 1992, Hanby preached at several of Jakes's conventions on topics such as Apostolic Order. Parsley, said a former Hanby associate, hired staff from Hanby's ministry and "preached eleven of Mark's sermons," in some places verbatim. According to the former Hanby associate, Hanby turned down Parsley's invitation to preach at his church. He told Parsley, "You need to be careful because you're making a fool of yourself, because there are thousands of people who know I preached that."[58]

Jakes, who already had transformed himself from a West Virginia country preacher to a Texas-based megastar, wrote the foreword to Hanby's 1996 book, *You Have Not Many Fathers*, in which he described Hanby as "a model of excellence and a mentor" and compared him to the Apostle Paul.[59] But this "model of excellence" had already declared bankruptcy, been in litigation with the IRS, and divorced his first wife.[60] He was also in business with Georgia attorney Dale Allison, who the following year was disbarred for falsifying documents to hide assets from members of the church of one of his clients, Calvin Simmons.[61] With Allison and others, Hanby helped to run a Bible school that was placed on the Texas Higher Education Coordinating Board's list of "fraudulent or substandard institutions" for purporting to offer college-level courses that were nothing more than "Sunday school lessons."[62] Hanby has continued to work with Allison, who also represented Parsley from the mid-1980s through the late '90s and has done legal work for Paulk and Long. Indeed, Long says Jakes is his "spiritual dad," and he credits Hanby as being a mentor who taught him "real kingdom theology."[63] Allison continues to serve on the board of Hanby's ministry and to operate other ventures the pair have launched together.[64]

Pearson, who said he knew nothing about Hanby's financial or personal problems, described him as "both a radical and a rascal." Hanby rebelled against the strict upbringing of the United Pentecostal Church (UPC), which was "the strictest sect of Pentecostalism that there is." Hanby had pastored one of the nation's first megachurches in Fort Worth in the 1980s, until the UPC kicked him out of the denomination for appearing on television.[65] Even today, the UPC rejects television as "being unsuitable for Christians or for their homes."[66] Like other Pentecostal denominations, the UPC emphasizes "holiness" over good works as the path to salvation and imposes strict rules of modesty on its followers. For example, it forbids swimming "in mixed company" and prohibits women from wearing makeup or pants, since "they immodestly reveal the feminine contours of upper leg, thigh, and hip."[67]

The former Hanby associate said that the abuse of the tithe is one of the reasons he no longer follows Hanby's teachings or works with him. "I think you need to have a relationship with people," he said, "instead of just take their money." The former associate said he was drawn to Hanby—by many accounts a gifted orator with radical insights into biblical teaching—because of Hanby's teaching on how the pastor should act as a father figure to his "sons" in ministry. He said he wanted to shepherd the next generation; instead he found that "the problem with most ministries today is they live for themselves and they die for themselves." According to the former associate, Hanby insisted on "spiritual authority," which was used to prevent congregants from questioning the pastor and to collect tithes. The pastors, he said, "live like kings." He added that Hanby emphasized authority more than any other concept in his teaching, drawing biblical analogies to David's reluctance to attack Saul because he knows Saul is the anointed one. "They basically use that as saying, if you come against, if you touch the anointed, you will die. Bad things will happen to you. And that's why people stay. Because they get brainwashed into this sort of thing. And it may not even be . . . conscious; it's just a subtle innuendo there." That brainwashing, he said, taps into people's desire to be part of something larger than themselves. "There's an incredible amount of spiritual manipulation and control, and part of it is that people want to be controlled. I mean,

I'm just as guilty as anybody else. We want to be part of something big, we want our lives to count, we want to impact the world, we want to change the world, we want to do great things."[68]

In a much less recognized way than Hagin and Roberts, Hanby has influenced the Word of Faith movement, too. Enabled by megastars like Jakes, Long, and Paulk, each of whom explicitly endorsed his teachings, and by culture warriors like Parsley, who adopted them, Hanby provided the spiritual muscle behind the authoritarian church structure that many prosperity preachers use to maintain control over their congregations—and their wallets.

THREE

God's Anointed Warriors

Today, as our president said in the moments after
9/11, we're going to get America on a war footing.
And I've come to the Mall today to tell the greatest
army of all time, the army of the living God, the
church of Jesus Christ, it is time to get on a war
footing!
—ROD PARSLEY, speaking at the America for Jesus rally
on the National Mall, October 22, 2004

In May 2005 Tony Perkins, president of the Family Research Council, made an appearance on TBN's *Praise the Lord* in which he introduced Rod Parsley to the audience as one of the "new generals" of a Christian army bringing a revival "in every realm of life." That Perkins was on TBN to introduce Parsley was a bit backward: Parsley, the flamboyant televangelist, was probably a better known figure by far to TBN's audience than Perkins, the political operative, was. But Perkins wasn't there to validate Parsley to the televangelist's audience. He was there to validate him to his own white conservative Christian base.

Perkins is a former Marine, Louisiana state legislator, founder of the ultraconservative Louisiana Family Forum, and Senate candidate. He also is one of the most powerful Christian right influence peddlers. Brought on to lead the James Dobson–founded Family Research Council in 2003, he is now more visible as an inside-the-Beltway player than Dobson is. Clean-cut, quick on his feet, and sharp-tongued, Perkins knows how to navigate the world of

Washington lobbying and politics; Dobson, the nerdy child psycholo-
gist, is given to whiney outbursts that have made him the target of
ridicule, such as when he complained that SpongeBob SquarePants
was turning kids gay. The audiences at Perkins-led events are evangelical, straight-laced, and mostly white.[1] Parsley's audience, by contrast, is charismatic, tongue-speaking, and racially diverse. By mid-
2005, when Perkins appeared on TBN, the distinction between
conservative evangelicals and their charismatic counterparts, at least
for political purposes, was fading. In 2004 Ted Haggard, the president
of the National Association of Evangelicals who later resigned in disgrace, said he found "no resistance to the Pentecostal-charismatic
message, and within 10 years, I don't know if there will be a distinction. I don't think the issue is theological; the issue is style."[2]

As Perkins's appearance on the garish, loud, and musical program
made clear, white evangelicals like himself—Perkins is a Southern
Baptist—are uncomfortable with the dancing, singing, and lavish display of charismatic gifts that take place on TBN. (Perkins half-joked
to host Tommy Tenney, "Don't tell my Baptist friends I was dancing.") But televangelists like Parsley not only have big churches; they
also have big television audiences that buy their books, tapes, and
DVDs. And for an operative like Perkins, for politicians like John
McCain or Sam Brownback, for political strategists like Ken
Mehlman or Karl Rove, reaching out to the Parsleys and the Hagees
is a calculated move to bring more voters into the fold of so-called
values voters, or the cultural conservatives they hope to turn into
Republican voters.

Referring to the televangelist as "General Parsley," Perkins and
Tenney turned Parsley's homophobic tirades, his hyperbole about
"activist judges," and his denunciations of "abortionists" into not
only a biblical imperative but a divinely-inspired act. Citing Romans
13, Perkins maintained that "government is a ministry. Government
is a mission field. . . . We need to send more Christians into government." Reflecting the "kingdom now" theology he adapted from

Hanby's teachings, Tenney analogized the anointing of a preacher with the anointing of a king. "If God can anoint a preacher to preach, he can anoint a king to rule, and we need people who will hear the call of God into government." General Parsley took the stage to let everyone know that in writing *Silent No More*, "the Lord was speaking very clearly to me."

In Parsley's parlance, every political showdown is a potentially earth-shattering, epic event. On the eve of a Senate vote on some of Bush's most controversial judicial nominees, Parsley warned that "it could be the defining day of our generation." To boost their claim that the government actually discriminates against godly Christians, Parsley and Perkins homed in on the nomination of Janice Rogers Brown. Brown was a controversial ultraconservative black California state court judge who decried the New Deal as "the triumph of our socialist revolution," who rejected civil rights laws, and who wrote that "where government advances—and it advances relentlessly—freedom is imperiled; community impoverished; religion marginalized and civilization itself jeopardized."[3] Despite her antigovernment rhetoric, Brown was ultimately confirmed for a seat on the United States Court of Appeals for the District of Columbia Circuit under the notorious Gang of Fourteen compromise that avoided the Republicans' use of a so-called nuclear option to block the Democrats' filibuster of her nomination.[4] On the eve of that compromise, Perkins falsely claimed that Brown "has some of the highest ratings from the ABA."

Although judicial nominations were the topic of the moment, Parsley wouldn't be satisfied merely with a conservative Christian takeover of the judiciary. Christian soldiers must take over every realm of public life to instigate a national revival. His movement included "anti-God" and " antichurch" public schools, popular culture, and media. Citing an Ann Coulter speech to the high school affiliated with his church, Parsley encouraged his young followers to "get in movies, get in TV, get in the secular press, become a national reporter, and stand up for righteousness." The right and duty of Christians to take over the government and society and replace secular institutions with biblical ones is the fundamental principle of dominionism,[5] and is a clear goal of Parsley and the other prosperity preachers.

But while Parsley insisted that he's no partisan—just a "Christocrat"—he offered highly charged partisan rhetoric cloaked in a biblical story. Complaining that a national revival didn't take place "because Ahab and Jezebel were sitting in the White House," Parsley made quite clear—to people tuned in to his biblical code words—that Democrats prevented his dream of a dominionist revolution from taking place. To many evangelicals, Hillary Clinton is like Jezebel, possibly the most evil woman in the Bible. It was Jezebel, married to Ahab, the king of Samaria, who forced her husband to turn his back on God and worship in a pagan temple where children were sacrificed—portending, for believers in biblical prophecy, that a future Jezebel would condone abortion. It was Jezebel who arranged for the death of a neighbor, Naboth, whose vineyard she and Ahab coveted; they then took possession of the vineyard. Jezebel is a wicked, domineering woman who controlled her husband. Although he had been morally corrupted, she was evil incarnate. Perry Stone, a biblical prophesier popular with Parsley and TBN, has compared Ahab and Jezebel's residence in an "ivory house" to the White House, Ahab and Jezebel's "land deal" to Whitewater, and the death of Naboth to the death of Vincent Foster.[6] Hagee drew the same comparison in *Day of Deception.*[7] Hagee has also blamed feminism on Jezebel, who controlled and manipulated her husband, killed the prophets, and "promoted the goddess cult."[8] Jezebel is also cited in the book of Revelation as evidence of satanic forces at work.[9]

Parsley's ten words, "because Ahab and Jezebel were sitting in the White House," then, were charged with meaning. The judicial nominee of the Republican president was on God's side. The

Democratic president was not, and, more important, the potential Democratic candidate was driven by Satan. With Perkins at his side, Tenney reacted to Parsley's rant by reinforcing the televangelist's purported divine inspiration: "How many of you think you are hearing from God right now, that God is speaking to you?"

General Parsley Conquers Ohio

Parsley's ambition has always been large. He claims to have started his ministry in his parents' backyard at age nineteen, preaching to seventeen people. His spiritual guidance came from the American evangelist Lester Sumrall, who passed his "sword of anointing" to Parsley before he died in 1996. In the foreword to Parsley's 1991 book, *Tribulation to Triumph: A Mandate for Today's Church*, Sumrall wrote that Parsley "puts his finger on the key to true victory in the Church, . . . holiness in our personal lives." Parsley also traces his theological lineage to the British evangelist Smith Wigglesworth, an itinerant preacher who claimed to have raised people from the dead. One of Parsley's favorite legends about Wigglesworth recounts how a woman wanted the evangelist to save her husband, but her husband was resistant to it. Wigglesworth slept in the couple's bed, and when he left (her husband still unsaved), he told the wife not to change the sheets. Parsley frequently repeats the story that the husband was saved by sleeping on the same sheets Wigglesworth had used, because the evangelist's anointing was on the sheets.[10]

Although Parsley publicly touts Wigglesworth's miraculous faith healing, behind closed doors evangelists admit it is just artifice. R. W. Schaumbach, a faith healer who appears frequently on TBN and at Parsley revival meetings, once told how he stood a body up against a wall in a morgue in an effort to replicate Wigglesworth's ability to raise people from the dead. According to someone who heard the story, "he put him up against the wall, and said, 'speak to me'; of course nothing happened. And he was joking about the fact of how hard it was to get this guy back on the slab. And he said, 'I don't tell that to my television audience.'"[11]

Parsley's foray into politics started out small and local. As his congregation grew in the 1980s, he launched ministries called Lifeline and Lightline, which crusaded against abortion and pornography. In 1986, Parsley was one of a group of ministers who successfully pressured officials to ban a gay rights group from distributing a safe sex pamphlet at the Ohio State Fair, because he feared children would be "recruited by homosexual groups in that immoral lifestyle."[12] His church youth group conducted a mock funeral for aborted fetuses outside a women's clinic in downtown Columbus,[13] and his church protested a local pornographic bookstore.

But as his ministry grew, Parsley concentrated on consolidating his television empire rather than on politics. His church was granted tax-exempt status by the Internal Revenue Service in 1985, and Parsley was ready to take in tithes and offerings from his growing congregation without having to disclose his finances to the public. His church and its nonprofit status were set up by Dale Allison, Hanby's business partner. According to Ole Anthony, Allison was one of several people traveling around the country in the 1980s and '90s who were showing churches "how to protect God's money from the government." Allison is described by sources in Georgia and in court records as a brazen con man who helped pastors set up dictatorial churches, through which they enriched themselves by convincing followers that God required them to give their money to the pastor. In 1997 Allison was disbarred for orchestrating bogus financial transactions with another preacher he represented, Calvin Simmons.

A person who was a member of Simmons's congregation and worked with Allison in the 1980s described the church as one that "used people beyond belief." According to this source, Simmons was a charismatic and persuasive man who looked like Clint Eastwood, and despite his lack of formal Bible training or college education, he held a few hundred people in his sway. Simmons's arrangement, said the former congregant, "couldn't happen without a crooked attorney," because having an attorney involved gave the operation the appearance of propriety. With Allison's help, Simmons created a church structure that demanded unquestioning obedience. They convinced the congregation—mostly people who were poor or of very modest means—that Simmons was a prophet of God. "If you went against the prophet," said the former congregant, "you would incur the wrath of God," a threat that caused "hurt and havoc" in people's lives.[14]

Although today Parsley admits he never graduated from college, his tax-exempt application to the IRS contains inconsistencies: he claimed to have attended Circleville Bible College from 1977 to 1981 and to have a bachelor of sacred literature degree from Logos Bible College in 1983. Circleville Bible College, now known as Ohio Christian University, refused to confirm the dates of his attendance, or the circumstances of his departure, and Parsley won't explain the discrepancy. Parsley's "degree" from Logos, if he has one, is hardly something to brag about, and he doesn't include it on his current profile. Logos was an unaccredited Bible college he ran out of his church basement in the 1980s while claiming that the college was accredited by the state of Ohio. When confronted in 1986 by angry students who discovered that their credits were not transferable, Parsley told the *Columbus Dispatch* that he was "very definitely a victim" of the Bible college's false claims. But Logos' lawyer was none other than Dale Allison—Parsley's own lawyer. Allison had prepared Parsley's tax-exempt application to the IRS and continued to represent him for at least a decade afterward. Allison and others had attempted to franchise Logos in other states as well; in Texas, with Mark Hanby, their efforts resulted in Logos being placed on the Texas Higher Education Coordinating Board's list of "fraudulent and substandard institutions."

Allison also drafted the bylaws that made Parsley the authoritarian ruler of his church. The corporate documents mandated that "it shall ever be understood that Rodney L. Parsley shall be a voting member for life, President of the Church Board for life, and Pastor of [World Harvest] Church for life. Any attempt by the Board members or officers to remove Rodney L. Parsley as a voting member, President of the Church Board, or as Pastor shall be void." The by-laws also permitted the pastor and ministerial staff to receive not only salaries but also housing allowances, auto expenses, and clothes cleaning expenses. Every member of the congregation was under a duty "to honor and esteem their Pastor; to pray for him fervently and daily; to attend constantly upon his ministrations; to manifest a ten-der regard for his reputation." These bylaws, according to the former Allison associate, conferred on the pastor "vast dictatorial powers" over his parishioners. World Harvest Church's bylaws claimed that "the government of the Church is in the hands of the Pastor, who has ultimate authority under Christ." That document also declared that "the church must function as a theocracy"; that a democracy "is not God's way"; and that "the purpose of the Church is not to do the will of the majority, but the will of God."[15]

Although Parsley was sued by church members and even family members in the mid-1990s, his ability to keep the details of those lawsuits secret allowed him to continue fund-raising and increasing his visibility through television. Continuing to ride the boost he got from Pearson's Azusa Conference, his television program, and his exposure through the sponsorship of other televangelists, Parsley was becoming more and more visible to neo-Pentecostals. His em-phasis was on driving out the satanic forces in a "sin-sick" society. In a 2000 appearance at Jakes's Manpower Conference, held at the forty-five-thousand-seat Tropicana Field in St. Petersburg, Florida, Parsley told the mostly black, all-male audience how to be a real man. He called on his listeners to be "remnant men," who "find a way to break through every line of Satan's defense." Remnant men, said Parsley, "have been divinely placed on the edge, . . . on the brink of a holy ghost revolution. They have come to the kingdom for a time such as this. . . . They have come to incite a riot, to affect a divine disturbance."

At the time, Jakes was a much larger figure among neo-Pentecostals than Parsley was. He had even caught the attention of his adopted state's governor, George W. Bush, who at the time of the Manpower Conference, was running for president. Jakes endorsed Parsley's call for a revolution, running and shouting on the stage as Parsley spoke in tongues, "slayed" people in the Holy Spirit, and claimed to cast out spirits of homosexuality, lust, incest, and sexual perversions amid the mayhem of men jumping, praying, and falling on the stage. Parsley claimed to read their minds as they thought: "something's happening to me while this white boy's preaching."[16] That something was sexual purity, rejection of vice, and casting out the devil, the elusive dream of God's puritanical kingdom on earth, which has been selling books, conferences, tithes, offerings, and television donations for Rod Parsley for nearly thirty years.

The period of early growth of Parsley's church—the late 1970s through the mid-1990s—saw the consolidation of power of the early leaders of the Christian right, like Jerry Falwell, Pat Robertson, and James Dobson.[17] And although Robertson displays charismatic gifts—particularly the gift of prophecy, however outlandish—and incorporated the prosperity message into his television broadcasts, the Christian right leadership remained largely white and evangelical, but not charismatic, for most of that period. Pastors of charismatic megachurches and TBN televangelists were not part of the political machine built by Dobson, Falwell, or Robertson, or by his protégé, the seemingly squeaky clean but morally corrupt Ralph Reed. As Doug Wead's detailed memos to George H. W. Bush made clear, the prosperity televangelism crowd was worth courting for votes, but steering clear of their peculiar shenanigans was highly recommended. By the time Bush's son—who had studied courting evangelicals at the knee of Wead—sought reelection in 2004, the entire conservative evangelical political apparatus had visibly embraced prosperity preachers as allies in the fight for the soul of America.

Riding a White Horse to the White House

In 2003 Roberta Combs, who was then president of Robertson's Christian Coalition, invited Parsley and his wife, Joni, to join her at a signing ceremony at the White House at which President Bush inked his signature on the partial-birth abortion ban. In Parsley's telling, that White House visit set his star rising among Washington religious conservatives. In his native Ohio, Parsley joined forces with Secretary of State J. Kenneth Blackwell in crisscrossing the state in support of the gay marriage ban, which was on the ballot during the 2004 presidential election. Undoubtedly, Blackwell's status as the co-chair of the state Bush-Cheney reelection campaign boosted not only the ban's chances but Bush's as well. In a blatant conflict of interest, Blackwell, in his capacity as secretary of state, also oversaw the election, which was riddled with inconsistencies, improprieties, and problems at polling places all over the state, but particularly in pre-dominantly Democratic, black urban areas.[18] After Bush won a second term when Ohio's electoral votes pushed him over the top, Blackwell—and Parsley—were credited with delivering Ohio to Bush.

Because 2004 was also the election of the vaunted values voters, Parsley began to present himself as not just Ohio's representative of those voters but as a national representative of "moral clarity." Just one month after the election, he was invited by James Dobson to an exclusive meeting of pastors to discuss bridging the divide between white and black churches; he subsequently became part of the Arlington Group, a coalition of leading religious conservative figures.[19] When Parsley promoted his book *Silent No More* in Washington, D.C., in 2005, he was the guest of Harry Jackson, an African American pastor from suburban Prince Georges County and a registered Democrat who supported Bush. Jackson, who has himself become a leading light of the conservative evangelical movement, working closely with the Family Research Council and appearing regularly on Christian talk radio with a sixty-second commentary, *The Truth in Black and White*, has high praise for Parsley.

Jackson said in 2005 that Parsley "is certainly on his way to having the appeal" that Robertson, Falwell, or Dobson have, but Parsley has the ability to "break the mold" because of his crossover appeal to blacks.[20] But Shelley Henderson, the former Bush White House staffer, said that in the black community, the churches of some white pastors with large black followings are considered "plantations" because the leadership of the church is mostly white. "I'm sure they love the Lord, I'm sure they're great churches, but I'm just saying there is some resentment about those kinds of churches. So I think that his may be one of those," said Henderson, adding, "I think a lot of people love him, too. . . . I think he's doing some good work for sure. But I think his church is one of those churches that may be looked up on as having maybe one or two token blacks in the leadership but by and large the leaders are white."[21] Nonetheless, Parsley's congregation is about 40 percent black.

Parsley has a fan club in the white conservative establishment as well. *Silent No More* was endorsed by Ted Haggard, who before his spectacular fall from grace after admitting to buying drugs from and meeting with a male prostitute, was a regular confidant of the White House. (After Haggard was forced out of his ministry, Parsley removed the dishonored pastor's endorsement from his Web site.) Ann Coulter made an appearance at Parsley's book launch in Columbus. And when Parsley came to Washington to promote the book to a mostly African American crowd at Constitution Hall, he appeared at a press conference in support of Brown's judicial nomination, along with Senator Bill Frist, then Senate majority leader, and Senator Jeff Sessions (R-AL).

Parsley's Center for Moral Clarity (CMC) functions as the political outreach of his church. He says he launched it "to affect moral change in our nation," based on the Bible, "the authoritative Word of God."[22] CMC's political director, Debbie Stacey, a Kansas-based anti-abortion activist who is married to a pastor in Parsley's ministerial fellowship, began arranging appointments with members of Congress as soon as Parsley launched the organization in 2004. Just one year after the televangelist founded CMC, Congressman Walter Jones (R-NC) said Parsley had been well-received by members of Congress because he "comes across as extremely sincere and dedicated" and "a humble servant."[23] In October 2005 both Jones and Senator Sam Brownback (R-KS) appeared at the launch of Parsley's other political project, Reformation Ohio. Jones flew to Columbus on the church's private jet, and the CMC paid for Brownback's travel and lodging.[24]

Through the CMC, Parsley has engaged in political advocacy on abortion, gay marriage, gambling, Terri Schiavo, judicial nominations, and Middle East policy.[25] He proposed criminalizing adultery,[26] and advocated for a bill introduced in the Ohio legislature that would ban abortion outright, an effort supporters hoped would eventually lead to a direct challenge to *Roe v. Wade*. He spoke at a press conference in support of the Houses of Worship Free Speech Restoration Act—which would lift the Internal Revenue Service ban on electioneering from the pulpit.[27] Also speaking were heavy hitters like Brownback, Senator Tom Coburn, Jones, Congressman Mike Pence, and political operator Jay Sekulow of the American Center for Law and Justice (ACLJ), whose colleague Colby May helped draft the bill. May also represents TBN, as does Dennis Brewer, an attorney who also staffs ACLJ's Texas office. Brewer has also represented TBN as well as some of the most notorious Word of Faith televangelists in both setting up their business structures and in civil and criminal litigation. Brewer has provided counsel to a range of televangelists, including Copeland, Jakes, and Paulk. He has also counseled the fallen, like W. V. Grant, who served prison time for tax fraud, and Tilton, who was exposed as a fraud on ABC's *Primetime Live*.

Parsley was included on White House conference calls about judicial nominations, advocated for the Supreme Court nominations of both John Roberts and Samuel Alito, and appeared at a controversial bill-signing ceremony with Texas governor Rick Perry. At the ceremony, held at a church on a Sunday morning, Perry signed a parental notification bill and gay marriage ban into law. Parsley, who appeared along with Perkins and American Family Association president Don Wildmon, called gay sex "a veritable breeding ground of disease."[28]

Although Parsley claims the CMC effort is nonpartisan, Zell Miller, the turncoat former Democratic Senator from Georgia, is the only Democrat to appear in conjunction with it. At an August 2005 gathering of over one thousand pastors at Parsley's church, Miller keynoted the event. Parsley grumbled that "when the IRS believes it has the right to tell me what I can say at the pulpit," the church is under "persecution." Thumbing his nose at the IRS, Parsley all but endorsed Blackwell, who was preparing to run in the Republican gubernatorial primary against two more moderate candidates. Turning to Blackwell, who was sitting in the room, Parsley declared, "I'm very proud to call you my friend."[29]

Two months later Parsley launched Reformation Ohio on the steps of the Ohio statehouse with Blackwell, Brownback, and Jones on hand. "It's an ambitious agenda," Parsley proclaimed, referring to his intention to register 400,000 new voters and save 100,000 Ohio souls. "It's a bold agenda. But it's an agenda demanded by our times and commanded by our God. . . . Man your battle stations, ready your weapons, lock and load. Let the reformation begin."[30] The same weekend, he hosted the Raise the Standard Conference for pastors, featuring Jones and Brownback as speakers, along with Alan Chambers of Exodus International, which claims to "convert" gay people to become straight, and Star Parker, founder of the Coalition on Urban Renewal and Education (CURE). Parker is a regular commentator on conservative television, radio, and Web sites and best summarizes her simultaneous conversion to Christianity and free-market conservatism in the title of her autobiography: *Pimps, Whores, and Welfare Brats: From Welfare Cheat to Conservative Messenger.*

Silent No More

By bringing his confrontational kingdom theology into politics, Parsley made himself a greater political presence—and liability—than any Word of Faith televangelist had to date. But that belligerence opened doors for his critics, who quickly homed in on his aggressive politicking on behalf of Blackwell, whose quest for the governor's mansion was seen as an effort to solidify Republican control of the state whose electoral votes had gone to the winner of all but two presidential elections for over one hundred years.

After a group of thirty Ohio clergy filed a complaint in early 2006 with the Internal Revenue Service, arguing that Parsley violated his church's tax-exempt status by his electioneering for Blackwell, Parsley denounced the complaint as baseless and politically motivated. Although he put an end to overt campaigning for candidates, he continued to insinuate himself into political issues and affiliate with Republicans. When Bush held a press conference to announce his support for a constitutional amendment banning gay marriage, Parsley touted how he was part of "a select group of nationally recognized Christian leaders," including Dobson and Charles Colson (the Watergate-felon-turned-prison-evangelist), who were invited to the event. "The fight for traditional marriage," said Parsley in typically grandiose terms, "is one of the epic battles of our generation."[31] CMC hosted a pastors and Christian leaders breakfast, featuring conservative talk radio personality Janet Parshall, an event that focused on advocating for a "national definition of marriage."

One of the corporate sponsors was InfoCision Management, a telemarketing and fund-raising firm that has profited handsomely from working for the Republican Party and has filled the party's coffers with campaign contributions made by its executives.[32] Info-Cision used a fund-raising ploy in 2003 on behalf of the National Republican Congressional Committee (NRCC), in which voters would receive a robocall from Tom DeLay informing them that they had just been nominated to a supposedly prestigious "business advisory council." If they agreed to participate, they were then asked to donate money to the NRCC as part of the honor. When the tactic was exposed in the *Washington Post,* campaign finance watchdog Fred Wertheimer said the method "fits into the hall of fame of telemarketing scams."[33] InfoCision, which also performs telemarketing services for several high-profile Christian right groups, did not respond to requests about whether it had performed such services for Parsley.

In the 2006 midterm elections, Blackwell was trounced by his Democratic rival, congressman and ordained Methodist minister Ted Strickland. The midterm election saw Republicans turned out of office all over the country, and in scandal-plagued Ohio in particular. Although Republicans maintained control of the legislature, Democrats took every statewide elected office, and the state's Republican junior senator was defeated by a progressive Democratic congressman, Sherrod Brown. Because of these and other Republican drubbings across the country, many observers saw the election not only as a repudiation of Bush-style Republicanism but also of the political operation known as the religious right—the carefully cultivated, generously financed, and cleverly intertwined web of think tanks, advocacy groups, grassroots organizations, lobbyists, lawmakers, churches, pundits, media outlets, and, most important, their precious values voters.

Yet in Ohio, as elsewhere, the picture was more complicated than that portrayal would suggest. Charles "Rocky" Saxbe, a Columbus attorney and prominent Republican, was part of a group of Republicans for Strickland who decried Blackwell's "intentionally divisive" religious rhetoric, especially on gay issues.[34] Saxbe's firm

nonetheless continued to represent Parsley, a longtime client for
whom Saxbe said he had "nothing but respect."[35] Parsley labored on,
despite the election results and the IRS complaint against him. His
candidate's failure and any legal proceedings against him are more
fuel for his fiery tirades about the persecution of Christians. His
2007 sequel to *Silent No More, Culturally Incorrect,* which blamed
Enlightenment thinking for the current cultural "battleground,"
made the *New York Times* best-seller list.[36] It was endorsed by Miller,
DeLay, Star Parker, Gary Bauer, Wildmon, Hagee, Falwell, and Paul
Weyrich, part of the old guard of the early religious conservative
(and mostly Catholic) political apparatus that had been under construction since the late 1970s. The white man who couldn't dance,
the "plantation owner," had become, in the words of the Religion
News Service, one of the country's top ten influential "kingmakers"
who are "shaping the Republican race for the White House."[37]

Stars of the Lone Star State

Like Parsley, John Hagee views his political mission in epic terms
and has long framed issues as battles between good and evil, or between Jesus' followers and Satan. From the start, his career has been
intertwined with people connected to Texas moneyed interests who
underwrite the infrastructure of the Texas Christian Right. Texas has
one of the best-funded and most powerful state networks of think
tanks and advocacy organizations, and that network has helped
boost the political fortunes of Bush, DeLay, and the dominant Texas
Republican Party.

At events at his Cornerstone Church in San Antonio, where the
five-thousand-seat sanctuary is often packed, at political rallies at
other churches, and even at the annual meeting of the American
Israel Public Affairs Committee, both Christians and Jews extol
Hagee. Shelley Henderson said that he "is well-loved in the African
American community. . . . He really is seen as someone who's very

genuine. . . . He's a major heavy hitter and so is really seen as someone who is sort of on the battlefield, very well respected. Everybody
loves John Hagee, for sure; he has credibility. So I think whatever he
is promoting would be well-received, certainly in the black community, . . . because people really trust him."[38]

Many of Hagee's early ventures, including the founding of his
nonprofit, Global Evangelism Television, in the early 1970s, were
started with the help of Charles Staffel, an accountant who later
went on to work closely with James Leininger, a wealthy San
Antonio businessman who earned his fortune from his company,
Kinetic Concepts, which sold specialty hospital beds. Leininger is
nicknamed the "sugar daddy" of the Texas Christian right because of
his generous funding of Christian right initiatives and the candidates
who backed them. His pet projects have included tort reform, private
school vouchers, and the teaching of Christian principles in public
schools, as well as hard-line hostility to reproductive and gay rights.
According to the Texas Freedom Network, a watchdog organization
that tracks the religious right, his efforts (and his money) have "been
instrumental in transforming the Texas State Board of Education
and the state Capitol into major battlegrounds in the nation's culture
wars."[39]

Leininger's largesse spreads far beyond Texas, however; his
Covenant Foundation is a major funder of Patrick Henry College, in
Purcellville, Virginia, which provides college training for home-
schooled kids to enter politics. Its students have worked as interns in
the Bush White House, and many of its graduates go on to work in
Republican politics.[40] The Covenant Foundation also funds Wall-
Builders, run by Republican Party operative and Kenneth Copeland
favorite David Barton.[41] Another recipient of Covenant funding is
the Illinois-based Institute for Basic Life Principles, a $63-million-a-
year enterprise that offers seminars in its authoritarian, biblically
based vision for government and society; the seminars are offered to
groups such as municipal governments and school boards, and in

America's prisons through a contract with the private prison giant Corrections Corporation of America.[42]

After serving as an executive for a number of Hagee ventures, Staffel went on to serve as an executive for Leininger at various organizations, including his Promised Land Dairy, which sells milk with Bible verses printed on the cartons; Focus Direct, a direct-mail firm that has served Republican candidates; the CEO Foundation, which gives money to Christian schools (including Hagee's) so poor children can attend them; the tort reform group Texas Justice Foundation and its political action committee (to which Hagee has donated money); and a Heritage Foundation clone, the Texas Public Policy Foundation, to name a few.[43]

Texas governor Rick Perry, who as a candidate received more than $1.3 million from Leininger in political contributions (and a much smaller amount from Hagee), is close with Hagee and has made appearances at his church. Leininger has also contributed generously to Senator John Cornyn (R-TX), also a Hagee ally and a recipient of campaign contributions from both Hagee and his wife. Leininger also contributed to the project of another powerful Hagee ally, Tom DeLay, with over $140,000 in donations to Texans for a Republican Majority, whose executives were later indicted for illegally laundering corporate campaign contributions.[44]

In 2002 Hagee participated in a Leininger-funded campaign designed to run moderate state Republican representatives out of office. The FreePAC, a hard-right political action committee funded largely by Leininger, Wal-Mart heir John Walton, and others involved in the effort to Christianize public education in Texas, targeted six moderate Republicans for defeat in the primaries. Hagee supported one of the FreePAC-backed state Senate candidates, state representative John Shields of the San Antonio area. (Even though pastors are barred by IRS rules from endorsing candidates from the pulpit, they can legally do so in their individual capacity.) In a letter to San Antonio–area voters, paid for by the Shields campaign and addressed to his "friends in Christ," Hagee wrote, "I'd like to lend my endorsement to John Shields." Calling his opponent, Jeff Wentworth, "the most aggressive pro-abortion politician in Texas" for his vote against a parental consent law, Hagee urged people to vote for Shields, "a committed Christian."[45]

Hagee's relationship with the Leininger family doesn't end there. Leininger's brother Peter, also a physician, founded the PAL Foundation, which doles out $100,000–$250,000 a year to Christian charities. Since 1998, PAL Foundation has given over $370,000 to Hagee's church and affiliated ministries.[46] Peter Leininger was also involved with Hagee in a failed business investment in a proposed hotel on the Riverwalk in downtown San Antonio.[47]

Sex, Secularism, and Satan

Hagee's early writings were focused on satanic forces in society, the coming Antichrist, and impending Armageddon—all themes that continued to figure prominently not only in his preaching but also in his political activity. In the 1970s, Hagee claimed to have received "shocking and unusual" revelations from God predicting the end of days, which would be immediately preceded by "persecution, spiritual and natural famine, denominational divisions, economic crisis, the arrival of a sociopolitical superchurch"—the Antichrist—"that will torment the Bride [of Christ], who may very well go underground in many areas and in some cases close the doors." Hagee predicted "mockery of great Christian leaders, evangelical doctrines in general" as the Antichrist takes over. The church's involvement in politics, said Hagee, "cannot save America, but the church united with prayer and fasting has the authority and power to control Washington, D.C., and every politician in it." With a swipe at churches that were involved in the civil rights movement and fighting poverty, Hagee maintained that "the clergy has promoted the war on poverty, urban renewal, Medicare, federal aid. They sign and circulate petitions for every issue except the right issue—Jesus Christ." The period's economic problems were, to Hagee, a sign of an economic collapse presaging the end of the world. He demanded that his followers invest their money not in the American financial system but in "a city whose Builder and Ruler is God."[48]

As Hagee became more political, he exhorted his followers to "take America back" from gay rights activists, abortionists, pornographers, and "secular humanists whose philosophy is Satan's theology in print." For Hagee, secular humanism, the New Age, and political correctness are all "intellectual idolatry, . . . nothing more than Nazism with a new mask." Hagee again excoriated the NEA as "anti-God and anti-family" and asserted that it had "transformed America's schools into social sewers, passing out condoms for diplomas. . . . They will give your teenage daughter a ride to the abortion clinic during school hours for an abortion without ever telling you." Hagee has attacked every conceivable conservative bugaboo, including the American Civil Liberties Union (ACLU) ("whose toxic thinking is nothing but intellectual cancer for America"); Norman Lear, Madonna, and Wilt Chamberlain (all "moral mongrels"); feminism ("the spirit of witchcraft"); and the occult (complaining that more people read Jeane Dixon's horoscopes than read the Bible).[49]

Spiritual warfare pervades Hagee's teachings. Aside from the good versus evil dichotomy, the epic battle between Jesus' army and Satan, the other epic war is between real Bible-believing men and limp-wristed atheists. The Bible, he says, "talks about becoming a part of the army of the living God. We are not a parade of patsies looking for an avenue of retreat. We are the army of Jesus Christ and victory is our heritage." In Hagee's pronouncements, "patsies" seems to refer to homosexuals, who are also treated to special scorn in Hagee's sermons, which are preached from the pulpit, and then turned into profit as he reprints and sells them in book, DVD, and CD form. He complains about "guilt trips" on taxpayers to pay for AIDS research and treatment, when it is caused by "your choice of behavior" and "sinful lifestyle." He has preached, "Listen up! I have a cure for AIDS, it's one hundred percent foolproof, and it's free: *stop fornicating.*" He complains that the military is downsized—not that it matters since he predicts there will be a nuclear war to bring about Armageddon—and blames it on Bill Clinton for making "the military the habitat of homosexuals by executive order. . . . The military will have difficulty recruiting healthy and strong heterosexuals for combat purposes. Why? Fighting in combat with a man in your fox hole that has AIDS or is HIV positive is double jeopardy."[50]

But gay men aren't the only patsies in Hagee's world. To "lazy louts, . . . full-grown men who are able to work," Hagee says, "I'd let them starve until their belly grew to their backbone before I gave them a dime." Hagee maintains that "you get it [money] by the sweat of your brow and you keep it by tithing and you increase it by sowing fertile seed into the Kingdom of God, until your harvest becomes a thirty-, sixty-, nintety-day harvest in the kingdom of God." If you're in bad financial shape, you shouldn't borrow money but sow what you have into the church. "If you borrow, credit will destroy you, that's what the book says."[51] Hagee condemns government assistance to the needy as against the word of God, quoting 2 Thessalonians 3:10, which says that if "a man won't work, he shouldn't eat."[52] Other patsies include "environmental wackos," whom Hagee describes as "overgrown Boy Scout[s] in green shorts with a backpack filled with trail mix. He is skipping along some nature path, communing with Mother Earth, humming when he stops to hug a tree."[53]

Real men are warriors, and real women submit to them. Like Parsley's intimation that powerful women are like Jezebel, Hagee maintains that "the feminist movement today is throwing off authority in rebellion against God's pattern for the family." God's plan, Hagee insists, "is for the wife to submit to the loving husband." Women who are "spirit-filled," he says, won't have a problem submitting. "But if you are controlled by the spirit of rebellion and the spirit of witchcraft and the spirit of carnality, . . . get ready for a fight."[54] He commands, "Wives, submit yourselves to your husbands," and complains that "the feminists of this country sold us a bill of goods that motherhood is a social disease." Proverbs 31, he says, "gives the portrait of an ideal woman. She is married, a mother, a homemaker, in her mouth is the law of kindness, and her husband puts his trust in her." Reiterating the common theme in authoritarian Word of Faith churches—that people who question the inerrancy of the pastor have a "rebellious spirit"—Hagee asserts that people don't read the Bible "because it convicts you of your sin and your carnality and your rebellious lifestyle. It is absolute rebellion against Jesus Christ to ignore his word."[55]

These views on men's and women's roles are not dredged up from the archives of Hagee's old writings. As recently as 2005, when he and his wife, Diana, published their book, *What Every Man Wants in a Woman/What Every Woman Wants in a Man*, Hagee advised women to "remember that your husband has a God-given role as leader of your home. Allow the Holy Spirit to help you willingly submit to his loving, godly leadership. Avoid the natural desire to manipulate his leadership and dominate in situations that arise in your family's life." The husband, says Hagee, "is the king, priest, and prophet" of his family.[56]

Hagee is no sexual prude; he calls the Bible "a book for lovers."[57] He relishes talking about sex, even once purring like a tiger at the thought of "get[ting] your motor running" by reading the Song of Solomon, which he called "the greatest sex manual."[58] Sex is God's idea, says Hagee, but "sex outside of marriage is absolutely forbidden. There are no excuses. God has zero tolerance for sex outside of marriage."[59] In the Pentecostal tradition in which Hagee grew up, sex within a second marriage is considered adultery. But Hagee never mentions his first marriage, even as he pines for the days when marriage was "until death do us part." Nor do he or Diana ever mention that two of the five children that they have repeatedly publicly claimed as theirs were the product of Hagee's first marriage. Hagee left his first wife when the children were one and four years old; he married Diana just six months after the divorce was final.[60]

Real men tithe to their church and follow the word of the Bible, which according to Hagee "is the only foundation on which America can build and survive" and provides the greatest financial counseling in the world. To emphasize the supernatural power of its blessing, Hagee added that "it will do for you what the phone booth did for Clark Kent."[61] But even when her husband is not abiding by the biblical imperative to tithe, the wife should still submit to his wishes, even though she knows his position is unbiblical. "I minister to many wives who are tormented by the fact their husbands refuse to give back to the Lord one-tenth of what the Provider has allowed them to earn," Diana Hagee writes. "A man who rejects the principle of tithing cannot understand the feelings of a woman who believes and trusts in the Word of God regarding prosperity." What to do, in Diana Hagee's view? The woman "knows that the Lord requires the tithe, . . . that he will provide blessings to those who obey the Lord with their tithe, . . . that the Lord promises to devour the enemies of her family when her family is obedient to the tithe." Yet obedience to her husband supercedes all of God's laws: "Based on the Word of God, she does not have many options. She must be obedient to her husband's decision."[62] A former member of Hagee's church said that Cornerstone's marriage counselors hewed to that philosophy: "If your husband was a big tither, and you had money, you were in the wrong. . . . But if he wasn't a good tither, and a big tither, leave him."[63]

Hagee believes there is one way that women do control their husbands: by their menstrual cycle. In an explanation of how husbands should respond to premenstrual syndrome, Hagee writes:

> Moods change dramatically, inexplicably, and instantaneously. On one day a man comes home, and his wife is waiting at the door dressed in a negligee with a rose in her teeth. He scoops her up in his arms, provided she doesn't weigh three hundred

pounds, and carries her off to the bedroom. He bangs on
his chest and yells like Tarzan, "It must be the cologne I'm
wearing!"

The next day . . . he races through the traffic and hurries
home for a repeat performance. Except she is not at the door
when he arrives. . . . Finally he spots her huddled in a chair in
the den crying her eyes out. He walks over and reaches to
comfort her, and she snarls like a half-starved junkyard dog,
"Don't touch me, you big ape. All you ever want is my body.
Sex, sex, sex, that's all you ever think about."

What happened? . . . Don't touch her, Bubba. If you do, you'll
get hurt. If she has PMS . . . you'll get killed.

Do you know the difference between a woman with PMS
and a snarling Doberman pinscher? The answer is *lipstick*. Do
you know the difference between a terrorist and a woman with
PMS? You can negotiate with a terrorist.[64]

When he fancies himself a Middle East policy expert, Hagee dismisses the possibility of negotiating with terrorists. But when he is an expert on matters of the heart, there is only one person less reasonable than a terrorist: a hormone-addled woman.

Christian Nation: Prophets for Profit

Throughout Bush's presidency, the prosperity preachers' involvement in politics only grew. Copeland—who had been courted by Bush's father and acted discreetly on his behalf—started giving sermons like "The Responsibility of a Righteous Vote" in which he described casting a vote as "a seed of faith." Like Parsley, he pretended to be nonpartisan, but he made statements like "no political party in the United States of America ought to stand for abortion" and "you can't make homosexuality right," and he hosted GOP operatives Barton and Butler on his television program. Like Hagee and Parsley, he delivered sermons that had almost nothing to do with policy and everything to do with epic struggles between good and evil, between the saved and unsaved. "We don't wrestle with flesh and blood, we wrestle with principalities and powers and rules of darkness of this world, that's not talking about people, that's talking about the devils that drive people."[65] But the overriding benefit of salvation, to Copeland, is prosperity.

Copeland is venerated in the Word of Faith movement. At the Assembly 2007, an event held in April 2007 to commemorate the settlement of Jamestown as evidence that America's founders intended it to be a "Christian nation," Copeland was the star attraction. Around the church where the event was held, John and Anne Gimenez's Rock Church in Virginia Beach, Virginia, that weekend, you could hear people speaking reverently about how Copeland preaches "the unadulterated word." As one follower told me, "He's just gifted to lead you down a path where anything's possible."

In Virginia Beach, John Gimenez introduced Copeland as "God's prophet, His servant," and "a man of God." Copeland, who once sent food back in a restaurant because "God doesn't want me to eat cold pancakes," was greeted with a reverential, enthusiastic, tongue-talking standing ovation. A youthful-looking seventy-year-old with glassy blue eyes, Copeland uses his good-ol'-Texas-country-boy storytelling yarns to humanize himself, but he revels in his followers' belief in his divine anointing. His rambling, disjointed sermon, which lasted over two hours, drew the largest crowd of the weekend, with thousands hanging on every word. Far-reaching, far-fetched, and hard to understand, it seemed to the audience to contain nuggets of wisdom—all from a college dropout who managed to build an empire around the idea that Jesus wants Christians to be rich.

Copeland parlayed his speech about America's Christian roots into what for him is the true meaning of Christ's spirit: becoming wealthy. Being saved, said Copeland, "instantaneously changed my thinking from that of a poor, in-debt, can't-do anything-right, complete and total failure in life to a wealthy man. . . . I have all the

money I'll ever need. . . . I have the blessing in my life." Because his
family believes in "the blessing," an all-encompassing concept that he
traces to God's covenant with Abraham and that rules his teachings,
Copeland claimed that his family has lived debt-free. A heart of un-
belief, he claimed, "is a wicked heart," but if you believe, you will receive the blessing. Pounding his chest, Copeland bellowed, *"I am
blessed!"* To the audience, uttering ecstatic murmurs and assents, he
advised, if you have problems in your own house (in other words, if
you're not blessed like me), "get rid of the evening news and the
newspaper" and instead study the "uncompromised word of the
Holy Ghost."[66]

The blessing also confers power, and Copeland urged his audience to "[take] control over principalities." Taking control over principalities is the fundamental principle of dominionism, which says
that the followers of Christ will control God's kingdom on earth.
Copeland's battle lines are clear: America, the Christian nation, is operated by politicians who "are necessary for paperwork," but believers in Christ "are the ones who are running this nation." Copeland
insisted that "we are a majority," adding that "two people and God is
a majority, anyway." It's the believers who have the blessing, who will
prosper, and will live debt-free. It's the believers who have dominion
over the earth and their finances and their health. Who needs doctors and banks and newspapers? All you need is the unadulterated
word.

America is at war with Islamofascists (Islamofascee-ists, as
Copeland called them), who are making an attack not on Western
civilization but "an attack on Jesus, it is an attack on him personally.
That means it's against you and me, and that means we have the
power and authority. . . . There's more to it than our military. . . . We
can rise up and take the day."[67] Christians can take the day if they
obey God. But if they don't obey God, bad things will happen. To
demonstrate this, Copeland has warned that Israeli voters have not
been obeying God, to dire consequences: "There are problems in

Israel's government today because they try to be like other nations. And when you do, you get people in there who don't know anything about the word of God and make wrong decisions and get your bus blown up. Same thing's true in our government."[68] In other words, America is not just any nation, it is Jesus' nation. Your belief otherwise—or reading the newspaper or listening to the evening news or putting your money in the bank instead of tithing—will reap more terrorism on our soil. Only the true Christians understand that, and they are armed and ready to combat it, with Copeland, Parsley, and Hagee as their battle commanders.

FOUR

World War III or the End of the World?

Those nations who align with God's purpose will receive His blessing. Those who follow a policy of opposition to God's purpose will receive the swift and severe judgment of God without limitation.
— JOHN HAGEE, *Jerusalem Countdown*

The carnival at Cornerstone Church in San Antonio looks, at first glance, like any other church festival, with rides, games, food, and children playing in the waning sunshine of a warm October afternoon. But look again and you'll see some unusual twists. The festivities are ringed with twelve booths selling food, each booth meant to signify one of the tribes of Israel. The booths, visitors are told, are in celebration of the Jewish holiday of Sukkoth. Under the tent, there's no preacher, no laying on of hands, no casting out devils. This tent houses a very different kind of revival, one in which Christians are buying challah covers, tallith, kiddush cups, mezuzahs, and other Judaic items, all made in Israel. They are buying products even though, as one woman remarked about the Hebrew writing, "I don't know what it says." Here on John Hagee's sprawling church property, on the weekend of Hagee's annual Night to Honor Israel, Hagee's followers from all over the country have come to celebrate what they call their "Hebraic roots" and to claim ownership of the world's most hotly contested piece of real estate: not for the Jews but for the Second Coming of Jesus Christ.

Inside the building, the entertainment is the stuff of biblical prophecy: stories of blood, gore, conflagrations, and apocalyptic showdowns between good and evil. Hagee's injection of the charged rhetoric of biblical prophecy into contemporary foreign policy has catapulted him to the forefront of an American Christian Zionist movement that has become the darling of conservative Israel hawks in Washington and neoconservatives yearning for regional war in the Middle East. This weekend former CIA director James Woolsey is a featured speaker, and Vice Prime Minister Shimon Peres of Israel will speak by video link. National and local Jewish leaders are on hand to pay homage to Hagee's alleged support for the Jewish people and the state of Israel. The Jews have no greater friend, the audience is told, than John Hagee, even though the book he wrote, prominently advertised on the church's parking lot marquee, predicts they will perish in a lake of brimstone at Armageddon.

The line for the Night to Honor Israel started forming outside the church even before the doors were scheduled to open. The atmosphere is festive, and people are filled with anticipation. But the party they are looking forward to is not taking place inside the church, where the Cornerstone Choir sings "Hava Nagila Texas Style!" and where, in a video montage of Jerusalem, the Dome of the Rock magically disappears. Rather, the anticipation is for the Second Coming, when, Hagee has said, Jesus will sit "right there on that Temple Mount" and rule the world.

Standing in line, people chat about what church they go to and which evangelists provide them inspiration. Behind me is a woman who introduces herself as Sharon, a gregarious public school reading teacher who looks to be in her midforties. A young African American man in front of us, a proud and enthusiastic member of Cornerstone ("I wouldn't go anywhere else"), thrills to the discovery that Sharon has just moved to San Antonio from Houston. "Did you go to Lakewood?" he asks hopefully, referring to Osteen's church.

Sharon did, but stopped going because she found it was "not spiritual enough" for her.

Like many people of her age I meet at charismatic churches, she grew up in a denominational church, in her case the Church of God, a Pentecostal denomination she describes as "very rules-oriented." Sharon is willing to tell me her spiritual life story, from her rejection of the strictness of her childhood church to her abandonment of church altogether as a young adult to her foray into Osteen's church. She became disaffected with that, too, and began studying and learning more about the Jewish roots of Christianity and attending Shalom Hebraic Christian Congregation in Houston. Sharon introduces me to her friend Cathy, another Hebraic Christian. A neatly dressed, soft-spoken woman about Sharon's age, Cathy used to attend Hagee's church and still supports the CUFI effort.

When the inevitable question about my church attendance comes, and I tell Sharon that I am Jewish, she gushes, "Praise God! Bless you!" I'm exotic to her, even though she considers herself to be Jewish. "Are you from the United States?" she asks me, as if an American Jew were an unimaginable novelty. (In my travels to Word of Faith churches, I have been asked that same question numerous times.) Sharon is breathlessly telling me about her experiences in dabbling with Hebrew when the doors open and we go through security. "Sit with us!" Sharon invites me, and I accept, because she is going to tell me about her particular walk with Jesus, whom she calls by his Hebrew name, Yeshuah Ha'Masiach.

As we walk into the sanctuary together, Sharon holds my arm and weeps as she describes how learning about Jewish customs such as kneading challah dough and attempting to participate in them has made her "feel closer to God." The setup at Cornerstone deliberately cultivates Hebraic Christianity; the five-thousand-seat sanctuary is flanked by both an American and an Israeli flag; twelve tapestries line the perimeter, each signifying one of the tribes of Israel, and congregants are divided into twelve "tribes." Couples married here receive a *katubah*, a Jewish marriage contract. Hagee claims to be teaching his followers Jewish customs so they will be ready when Jesus, a rabbi, comes back.

Sharon feels certain she had Jewish ancestors, because "I knew how to daven even before I knew what davening was!" (*Daven* literally means "to pray" but is often associated with bending and bowing at particular points in the prayer.) But while Sharon seems to revel in Jewish traditions, Cathy tells me that she is "motivated to study and align with Jews" and "study her Hebrew roots" so she can be "part of the House of Israel" in preparation for the end times. Citing the book of Ezekiel, Cathy tells me earnestly that "the Father is bringing us together. . . . The power of the Holy Spirit is gathering the remnant." In both the Old and New Testaments, she adds, "God left a remnant of people to carry on." Cathy wants to be part of the remnant.

The remnant, according to Hagee and others, will consist of evangelists who resist the persecution of the Antichrist to preach the gospel to nonbelievers during the Tribulation. Christian believers in end-time prophecy trust that when the Rapture takes place, all believers will be whisked off to heaven so they will not have to endure the hardship of the Tribulation. In the 2000 film *Left Behind*, based on the blockbuster novel by Tim LaHaye and Jerry Jenkins, Hagee and his wife are seen disappearing from an airplane during the Rapture. But end-timers also believe that the book of Revelation predicts that there will be a remnant—modern-day apostles—who remain on earth to resist the temptation of the devil "and have the testimony of Jesus Christ."[1] In Hagee's own 1999 docudrama, *Vanished*, viewers are told that during the Tribulation there will be 144,000 evangelists who will "show you the truth" while the Antichrist is consolidating his hold over his one-world order. Only those who follow the remnant—along with those who were whisked away during the Rapture—will survive the final showdown between

Christ and the Antichrist at Armageddon to live under Christ's rule at the Second Coming.

The remnant, Hagee maintains, will be persecuted by everyone else, who will have fallen under the spell of the false prophet, the Antichrist. Hagee believes that the Antichrist will institute a one-world economic system, government, and religion. Hagee has believed for years that debit cards and other conveniences of modern banking are evidence of a one-world economic system coming into existence. Proof of the one-world government includes the United Nations and the World Health Organization, and evidence of the one-world religion includes the American Bar Association, hate crimes legislation, and the fact that the Ten Commandments are not taught or displayed in public schools.[2]

The supposed persecution of Christians—a favorite narrative of the conservative evangelical Christian movement—is evidence to Hagee that the end-times are fast approaching. *Vanished*, in which Hagee's sermonizing is interspersed with a *War of the Worlds*-style depiction of the end of days, replete with "newscasts" reporting on events, shows that during the Antichrist's rule, Christians will be "hunted down and arrested," that jails will be "filled to the brim" with them, and Bibles will be burned.

Hagee makes clear that the Jews will be left behind on earth at the time of the Rapture and will have to be brought to Christ to survive the final showdown at Armageddon. "The Jewish people, in part, have been blinded to the identity of the Messiah temporarily," Hagee writes in *Jerusalem Countdown*. "A deliverer shall come out of Zion and take away the sins and ungodliness of Jacob, meaning the Jewish people. . . . That 'deliverer out of Zion' is none other than Jesus Christ of Nazareth."[3] This is not a new narrative for Hagee; in 1995 after Israeli prime minister Yitzhak Rabin was assassinated by a Jewish extremist, Hagee wasted no time in penning his *Beginning of the End: The Assassination of Yitzhak Rabin and the Coming Antichrist*, the best seller in which he maintained that the Second Coming is "the most important truth of our age—not merely to understand but to anticipate, embrace, and live out." The shot that killed Rabin, Hagee insists, "launched biblical prophecy onto the fast track" because it galvanized Israelis in support of the peace process, which, in Hagee's view, is contrary to the word of God.[4]

The peace process itself, then, was evidence to Hagee that the Antichrist is appearing, since the Bible predicts that the Antichrist will usher in a period of false peace before the ultimate Second Coming of Jesus. He intimated that the Antichrist might be then-president Bill Clinton, who was negotiating peace agreements between Israel and the Palestinians: "We also know that the Antichrist will enter the world stage with a reputation of being a powerful man of peace. . . . He will defeat and merge three kingdoms—could they be Serbia, Bosnia, and Croatia? . . . He will guarantee peace for Israel and the Middle East [but] . . . his peace is neither eternal or true."[5]

Preparing for her role as part of the remnant, Cathy seeks to follow God's commandments so she can make it there. "Bad things will happen to America," she tells me, if America doesn't follow God's commandment in Genesis 12:3 to bless Israel. She leans over Sharon, who is sitting between us, and asks me, over the strains of the Cornerstone Choir playing Jewish folk songs, if I know why Hurricanes Katrina and Rita had taken place. No, I don't know, I say. "The Gaza land giveaway," she replies, fixing her blue eyes on mine. The roadmap for peace, she adds, was against God's word and will bring bad things to America.

Cathy used to attend Hagee's church but doesn't any longer. She tries to observe Shabbat ("I don't go shopping or anything, I just hang out") and she is "tired of" celebrating Christmas and Easter. "He [Hagee] could be going further in observing the feasts," she says. I know what she is talking about only because I attended Hagee's morning service that day. He sermonized about what he calls the Seven Feasts, a strange retelling of five Jewish holidays to predict the Second Coming of Christ. As is common with Word of

Faith prophesiers, he merges the New and Old Testaments, suggesting that the Old Testament contains predictions of Christ's birth, life, death, and resurrection. But at the heart of it all is money, as Hagee insists that "the feast of the first fruits" requires the tithe.

Armageddon: Joy for Goys

"How many of you have come to the House of the Lord with your tithes and offerings this morning?" he demands, humiliating anyone who didn't raise their hand. He tells his congregation to "present the first fruits to the King of Kings, the Lord of Lords." In explaining what the first fruit is, Hagee makes clear that the tithe is the first thing one should pay—before the rent, before the credit card bills. If you pay your bills first and then tithe, says Hagee, "this is not first fruits. That's giving God what's left." Giving God the leftovers, Hagee says later in the sermon, is a sin, and the reason why your finances are in trouble. "You're stealing your tithes from God right now," he warns. "You're living under a financial curse, the Bible says that. You're not giving God the first fruits." Like almost all Word of Faith mythology, the agrarian society depicted in the Bible is transformed into a twenty-first-century moneymaking scheme. In the same way that mainline Christians find Word of Faith a distortion of the New Testament, Word of Faith also distorts the Old Testament for its own profit motive.

The "seven feasts" described by Hagee are not readily recognizable to any mainstream Jew, and most Christians would likely be mystified as well. Because the Jewish holidays will be celebrated during Christ's millennial reign, "the golden era of peace when Messiah comes," Hagee claims to be preparing his followers to be active participants. "I want you to have this so that when the other Gentiles are stumbling around in the dark and asking a thousand stupid questions, you will not be numbered among them." In other words, the celebration of the Jewish holidays is not about loving the

Jews, it's about getting ready for Jesus. And his audience is as ready
and willing as if he were inviting them to a party or a football game.
Hagee once told Copeland that he takes his church members to
Jerusalem "to get them familiar with what the land looks like and the
customs of the people, because this is what's going to be for one
thousand years when Jesus sits right there on that Temple Mount,
and sits on the throne of his father David, and you're going to see
presidents and prime ministers and queens lined up in a long line to
kneel at the feet of the son of God, the son of a Jewish carpenter, the
king of kings. . . . Right there, you're going to see that with your eyes
someday."[6] No wonder, then, that the Dome of the Rock, a holy
shrine for Muslims, conveniently evaporated from Hagee's dramatic
video footage of the holy city.

The first feast, says Hagee, is Passover. The message of Passover
for Hagee is "redemption by blood, the cornerstone of Christian
teaching." (For Jews, the message of Passover is freedom from slavery; the blood represents the animal sacrifice to stop the pharaoh
from killing the Jews' first born, not the Christ-like redemption that
Hagee is claiming.) The next feast is what Hagee calls the "Feast of
Unleavened Bread," also known to Jews as Passover. But Hagee
views the unleavened bread not as the expediency required by the
Jews' Exodus out of Egypt but as a symbol of "arrogance and pride."
The message of the "unleavened bread is that God has zero tolerance for sin," which is why, Hagee claims, the Old Testament requires
Jews to clean their houses of every crumb of leavened bread before
Passover. The housecleaning required of observant Jews is actually
based on rabbinical teaching rather than on the Torah itself, but that
is of no moment to this friend of the Jews. The third feast he spins
out of Passover is the "Feast of the First Fruits," in Judaism a celebration of spring, which Hagee uses to wrench people's hard-earned
money out of their hands before they can even pay their bills.

Hagee's sermon is rambling, but it is met with applause, amens,
and praise. He meanders to the other "feasts," the next one being

Pentecost, the period during which Christians believe Christ rose from the dead, "a long interval that typifies dispensation of grace in which the Holy Spirit is gathering the church to rapture." Jews, of course, do not celebrate the Pentecost but do celebrate Shavuot at that same time—fifty days after Passover. But to his charismatic audience, the reference to the Pentecost is of utmost significance, because that was when believers were filled with the Holy Spirit. The rest of the "feasts" are massaged to fit into Hagee's prophecy about the Second Coming: the "Prophecy of the Trumpets," known to Jews as Rosh Hashanah, represents the "regathering of the church," because to Hagee, the blowing of the shofar announces Christ's imminent return. The "Prophecy of Atonement," known to Jews as Yom Kippur, is known to Hagee as Judgment Day. And the "Prophecy of the Tabernacles," known to Jews as Sukkoth and supposedly celebrated at Cornerstone that weekend, is the time at which Hagee claims Christ will rise again.

All of this hurtling toward Armageddon is supposed to bring his congregants joy, Hagee maintains. "The world is sick of mule-faced Christianity," he complains. The feast of the tabernacles, he maintains, "is a season of joy.... There is a sad lack of contagious joy in churches in America." Hagee asks: "How many of you have lost your joy?" Thousands of people in the sanctuary raise their hands. "Ask the Lord into your life," says Hagee, while people murmur their commitment to follow Hagee, a taciturn man who rarely smiles. "There is divine joy at the Feast of Tabernacles!"

The ultimate goal, as the Hebraic Christians I talked to that day made clear, is not to be Jewish but to prepare for the end of days when Jesus—or Yeshuah—will return. Although Christians will hail his appearance as a return, Hebraic Christians believe Jews will understand the second time around, and they will see that the Second Coming represents the Messiah they have been waiting for. Hagee believes that, too, as he writes in a 1996 book: "Jesus Christ, the Messiah for Jews and Gentiles alike, first came to earth nearly two thousand years ago. He will come to earth again when he steps foot on the Mount of Olives just outside Jerusalem."[7] Hagee's Jewish defenders insist that he does not aim to convert Jews to Christianity. But Hagee's followers are latched onto his promise that the end is nigh—perhaps while you are reading these words—and that anyone who is not a believer in Christ as their savior will not survive it.

Christians United for Profit

In its short history, Hagee's grassroots movement, CUFI, has become the most visible organization of American Christian Zionists. Hagee launched the organization in February 2006, just a month after the release of his book *Jerusalem Countdown*, which became a best seller. In the book Hagee asserts that an American and Israeli war on Iran is not only biblically prophesied but necessary to bring about Armageddon and the Second Coming, a theme that drew four hundred pastors and Christian leaders to San Antonio to the inaugural meeting of his Christian Zionist organization.

Many of the attendees were televangelists well-known for their Word of Faith preaching on TBN. Benny Hinn, Kenneth Copeland, Joyce Meyer, Jesse Duplantis, and Mac Hammond were there, as was Stephen Strang, president of Strang Communications. (Strang Communications is publisher of *Charisma* magazine, the leading magazine in Word of Faith and charismatic circles, and the umbrella organization for numerous publishing imprints, one of which published Hagee's book.) A strong supporter of Bush and the Iraq War, Strang has said that many times when a pastor launches a new organization, "second-tier" figures show up in support, "because everyone's busy, and everybody's busy with their own agenda, . . . but this, in my opinion [was] pretty top level."[8] Others, like Parsley and Hagin, did not attend the launch but signed on later for leadership roles in the organization. Many of them, including Strang, Hammond, and Duplantis, were on hand for the Night to Honor

Israel weekend festivities in 2006; Parsley and Jakes agreed to speak at the 2007 event.

CUFI shows how Word of Faith melds with conservative evangelicalism, movement conservatism, and the GOP. Janet Parshall, the popular conservative talk radio host, was at the launch and signed on to the board of advisers. Gary Bauer, the former Bush Sr. White House aide and Republican presidential candidate, and George Morrison, the former chairman of the man-centered Promise Keepers, are on CUFI's executive committee, as was Jerry Falwell before his death. The organization's executive director, David Brog (who is Jewish), is a former chief of staff to Senator Arlen Specter (R-PA).

An evangelical pastor from Colorado, Morrison is a long-time ally of Hagee's in the Christian Zionist movement. Speaking just two months after the 2006 CUFI launch, Morrison predicted that although prior efforts to create a unified grassroots Christian Zionist movement had stumbled, CUFI would gain steam because of the escalating tensions with Iran and the recent election of the Hamas-led Palestinian government. Morrison said that "almost every evangelical organization that I know of" was present at the CUFI launch, "a tremendous turnout." Hagee, said Morrison, "has the platform, his TV ministry, . . . he has the great respect of a lot of other leaders, so certainly, he's in that position . . . of spiritual leadership and authority to lead the evangelical churches and help unite them" around CUFI.[9] Hagee has claimed that he has a mailing list of two million people, and the twenty thousand "spiritual leaders" on his list all forward his e-mails to their own supporters, who in some cases have their own lists of a million people.[10]

Islam: The Enemy

The launch of CUFI around the time of the release of Hagee's book undoubtedly propelled sales and helped hype a case for war against

Iran. By April 2006, two months after CUFI's launch and three
months after its release, the book had sold over 620,000 copies.
Some of the sales are accounted for by the fact that ministries like
Hagee's will buy books in bulk, then give them as "gifts" as part of
fund-raising campaigns.[11] But even apart from sales directly to ministries and churches, the book ranked twenty-first on *USA Today*'s
best-seller list and topped the *Publishers Weekly*'s religion best-seller
list, Wal-Mart's inspirational best-seller list, and the Christian Book-
seller's Association (CBA's) best-seller list.[12]

Hagee's long-standing view that "Jerusalem must remain undi-
vided as the eternal capital of the Jewish people" (meaning no portion of it should be turned over to the Palestinians) has made him
popular with neoconservative hawks. One Jerusalem, an organization committed to that principle, has embraced Hagee's CUFI effort.
One Jerusalem was founded by, among others, Douglas Feith, who
became Bush's undersecretary of defense for policy and notoriously
peddled in cherry-picked intelligence to push the case for the war
against Iraq, and Natan Sharansky, the former Soviet dissident and
Israeli government official.[13] Bush admires Sharansky's writings and
awarded him a Presidential Medal of Freedom in 2006.[14]

On the Saturday before his Night to Honor Israel, with his audience dotted with Christians wearing tallith and yarmulkes, Hagee
hosted his Middle East Intelligence Briefing, billed as insider information not available anywhere else. James Woolsey, the former CIA
director, thrilled the crowd when he pronounced Israel an essential
ally in the war against Islamic fanaticism. But he bewildered it with
his suggestion that to see who might be aiding terrorists they should
look in their rearview mirrors when they fill their cars up with gas.
(The parking lot outside was filled with gas-guzzling SUVs.) Other
speakers lent a distinctly anti-Muslim shrillness to the afternoon,
less a diatribe against terrorism and more an indictment of Islam.
Brigitte Gabriel, a Lebanese Christian who survived the turmoil of
the Lebanese civil war in the 1980s, gave a fevered, vindictive

speech about why she supports Israel. (No Muslim was ever nice to her, and Israeli soldiers saved her from starvation.)

Gabriel, author of the book *Because They Hate: A Survivor of Islamic Terror Warns America,* attempts to draw parallels between her experience in Lebanon and an Islamic threat to American democracy. When Muslims became a majority in Lebanon ("they multiply much more quickly than we do"), Christians were "attacked for tolerance, open-mindedness, and multiculturalism." (At the same time, Gabriel derides "political correctness" as ignorant and dangerous.) Gabriel added that "because we are Christians, Muslims want to kill us." In contrast, she went on (conveniently not noting Israeli-led atrocities against civilians during the same period), "Jews showed compassion in a way that Muslims didn't."

Gabriel also runs the Virginia Beach–based American Congress for Truth, whose board of advisers is stacked with inside-the-Beltway neoconservative hawks often featured in print and broadcast conservative media outlets: Kenneth Timmerman, founder of the Foundation for Democracy in Iran and author of the book *Countdown to Crisis: The Coming Nuclear Showdown with Iran;* Harvey Kushner, author of *Home Front: The Secret Islamic Terror Network in the United States;* Walid Phares, senior fellow at the neoconservative Foundation for the Defense of Democracies and a critic of withdrawal from Iraq; as well as Woolsey himself. The founding principles of ACT sound like a Rush Limbaugh playbook, as the organization aims to "give Americans their voice back. That unique American voice, full of joy and anticipation of better days and infinite aspirations . . . muted by the scourge of political correctness. We are now a society neutered by this scourge, . . . unable to act or speak for fear of offending, or of lawsuits, or of accusations of one-sided political views. Millions either do not realize, or deny the threat of militant Islam to America, Israel and all of Western civilization."[15]

To Hagee's audience, Gabriel, a regular on the conservative talk radio circuit, claims that Hamas has cells in all major American cities and that Hezbollah has eleven cells in the country, one with a general who was smuggled over the U.S.-Mexico border. She tells heartbreaking tales of her family's dire brushes with starvation and death during the bloody civil war, but her disdain for all things Muslim and her deification of all things Jewish is hysterical and bizarre. Nevertheless, the more she implores Hagee's audience to love the Jews because a group of Israeli soldiers rescued her from Muslim fanatics, the more they adore her. She gets a huge standing ovation (and a hug from Woolsey) after imploring the receptive audience to "throw political correctness in the garbage where it belongs!" Gabriel, an immigrant who became a U.S. citizen, once told Hagee that America's "immigration problem" mirrors the problem Lebanon had that led to its "fall to radical Islamic forces." Gabriel further claimed that al Qaeda and Hezbollah are working with the Salvadoran MS-13 gang in the United States. "Not only are we inviting our enemy in, but this enemy is coming into the United States, marrying American citizens who are Muslims who are sympathizers of Hezbollah terrorists, and producing more children. . . . There is going to be a severe crisis in the near future because America has allowed a policy of open borders."[16]

Christians United for War

Jerusalem Countdown, Hagee's manifesto for war with Iran, provides a peculiar mix of biblical prophecy, purported inside information from Israeli government officials, and a mixed-up, pared-down lesson in nuclear physics. "I wrote this book in April 2005, and when people read it, they will think I wrote it late last night after the Fox News report," Hagee has said, without a trace of irony. "It's that close to where we are and beyond."[17] But the particulars of Iran's nuclear program do not seem to interest Hagee. In many of his television and radio appearances in early 2006, he glossed over the obstacles faced by Tehran in creating a viable nuclear weapon, arguing that "once you have enriched uranium, the genie is out of the bottle."[18] In March 2006 he claimed that within a month, "Iran will have the nu-clear—the enriched uranium to make the—have the nuclear capabil-ity to make a bomb, a suitcase bomb, a missile head, or anything they want to do with it."[19] So when the Iranian president announced the following month that Tehran had enriched uranium (although not enough to make a bomb), Hagee claimed—despite prevailing scientific opinion to the contrary—that the Iranians "now have en-riched uranium that will lead to the production of nuclear suitcase bombs designed to destroy American cities with one blast. These nu-clear weapons will also be used against Israel." To fully emphasize the need for war, Hagee added, "the question is not if there will be a military preemptive strike against Iran. . . . The question is when."[20] To prime his followers for such a possibility, Hagee has argued that Iran's development of nuclear weapons must be stopped to protect America and Israel from a nuclear attack. He has also warned of a supposed Iranian-led plan to simultaneously explode nuclear suit-case bombs in seven American cities, or to use an electromagnetic pulse device to create "an American Hiroshima."[21]

His rhetoric is directed not only at his audience of believers but also at a broader audience, whose justifiable nervousness about ter-rorism he seeks to exploit. Hagee was for months comparing Mahmoud Ahmadinejad to Hitler—still a favorite rhetorical device—before Seymour Hersh informed the reality-based world that the Bush administration, too, was talking up the confrontational, Holocaust-denying Iranian president as the next führer. In early April 2006, Hersh reported that "Bush and others in the White House view him as a potential Adolf Hitler, a former senior intelli-gence official said. 'That's the name they're using. They say, 'Will Iran get a strategic weapon and threaten another world war?'"[22]

Hagee seems to delight in a coming confrontation. He argues that a strike against Iran will cause Arab nations to unite under Russia's leadership, as outlined in chapters 38 and 39 of the book of

Ezekiel, leading to an "inferno [that] will explode across the Middle East, plunging the world toward Armageddon."[23] During Hagee's appearance on Benny Hinn's program, Hinn, who frequently predicts the end is imminent, enthused, "We are living in the last days. These are the most exciting days in church history." The master of signs and wonders then went on to add, "We are facing now [the] most dangerous moment for America." At one point, Hinn clapped his hands in delight and shouted, "Yes! Glory!" and then urged his viewers to donate money faster because he is running out of time to preach the gospel.[24]

Hagee's book, and his discussion of it in Christian media outlets, is absolutist. He speaks not only of good against evil, believer against nonbeliever, Judeo-Christian civilization against Islamic civilization, but also of an American-Israeli alliance against the rest of the world. He plays on conservative disdain for anything European while promoting the Bush unilateralist mentality that has had catastrophic results in Iraq. He expresses contempt for diplomacy, calling the UN Security Council "a joke." Rabbi Daniel Lapin, the Orthodox rabbi who once worked with convicted lobbyist Jack Abramoff, said after a Purim appearance on TBN with Hagee that "Pastor Hagee has a very realistic understanding of the United Nations . . . and recognizes it as unlikely to be any more helpful in this looming tension than it has been in any other in the past."[25] He paints Russia and China as America's enemies, claiming, without basis, that Russia has helped Iran build long-range missiles that could reach New York City.

In Hagee's telling, Israel has no choice but to strike at Iran's nuclear facilities, with or without America's help. The strike will provoke Russia—which wants Persian Gulf oil—to lead an army of Arab nations against Israel. Then God will wipe out all but one-sixth of the Russian-led army, as the world watches "with shock and awe," he says, lending either a divine quality to the Bush administration phrase or a Bush-like quality to God's wrath.

But Hagee doesn't stop there. He adds that Ezekiel predicts fire "upon those who live in security in the coastlands." From this sentence he concludes that there will be judgment upon all who stood by while the Russian-led force invaded Israel, and he issues a stark warning to the United States to intervene: "Could it be that America, who refuses to defend Israel from the Russian invasion, will experience nuclear warfare on our east and west coasts?" He says yes, citing Genesis 12:3, in which God said to Israel: "I will bless those who bless you, and I will curse him who curses you."

To fill the power vacuum left by God's decimation of the Russian army, the Antichrist—identified by Hagee as the head of the European Union—will rule "a one-world government, a one-world currency and a one-world religion" for three and a half years. (He adds that "one need only be a casual observer of current events to see that all three of these things are coming into reality.") The "demonic world leader" will then be confronted by a false prophet, identified by Hagee as China, at Armageddon, the Mount of Megiddo in Israel. As they prepare for the final battle, Jesus will return on a white horse and cast both villains—and presumably any nonbelievers—into a "lake of fire burning with brimstone," thus marking the beginning of his millennial reign.[26]

Twenty-first-Century Churchill?

By the summer of CUFI's first year, Hagee, long cozy with Bush and other Republicans, surely had demonstrated his spiritual and political authority, not only among his fellow evangelicals but also inside the Beltway. At the first CUFI Washington Summit in 2006, attended by 3,500 members, banquet speakers included then-senator Rick Santorum, Senator Sam Brownback, and then–Republican National Committee chair Ken Mehlman. President Bush sent his video greetings. Some Democrats—all Jewish—also spoke at the CUFI banquet. The next day, at a White House ceremony at which Bush vetoed a bill to fund stem cell research, Karl Rove overheard Santorum and

Brownback discussing the event and asked to find out more about it.[27] Parsley, who had attended the CUFI summit, was also at that veto ceremony.[28]

Hagee, Brog, and a handful of other CUFI leaders garnered a White House meeting with Deputy National Security Adviser Elliot Abrams in which, according to Brog, "we shared our views. On all of our three talking points."[29] The talking points included advocating Israel's continued antiterrorism activities in Gaza and Lebanon; blocking aid to Hamas; and preventing a nuclear Iran. The meeting took place during that summer's Israel-Hezbollah conflict, and CUFI was active in advocating against a cease fire, urging its grassroots members to barrage the White House with telephone calls.[30] Brog added, "I think we're becoming an organization with some say in Washington. . . . I think we're getting influence as far as Middle Eastern policy."[31]

Hagee was also influencing the rhetoric of nascent presidential campaigns. As CUFI descended on Washington and the bloodshed at the Israel-Lebanon border raged, John McCain and Newt Gingrich took to the airwaves to proclaim the beginning of World War III. Their comments, Knesset member Benny Elon told the *Jerusalem Post*, had their roots in Hagee's book. As tourism minister, Elon led the Israeli government's outreach to evangelicals and advocated expulsion of Palestinians from the occupied territories.[32] Five months later, he presented Hagee with an award from the Knesset Christian Allies Caucus. In giving Hagee the award, the caucus said it was "committed to bringing to the attention of the people of Israel the unqualified support Christians have given and continue to give to the welfare and security of the Jewish people."[33]

Gingrich and McCain invoked the World War III terminology, Elon told the *Jerusalem Post* in July, "because they think it will lead to Iran getting involved, which they believe will set off World War III."[34] In addition to Gingrich and McCain, who singled out Iran as the provocateur in the coming epic war, neoconservative William

Kristol echoed those same sentiments in a column in his *Weekly Standard.* Kristol called Iran "the prime mover" behind an "Islamist war" against "democratic civilization."[35]

While Hagee spent CUFI's first year drumming up support for a war with Iran, Brog was playing down Hagee's incendiary rhetoric about world-ending confrontations between good and evil. When asked about Hagee's view of the possibility of a diplomatic solution to the standoff regarding Iran's nuclear program, Brog said, "I think he'd agree, if there were diplomatic ways of avoiding it, by all means. I think he'd agree we need to take certain steps. But I think he'd also recognize that there hasn't been a great response, that Ahmadinejad doesn't seem amenable to these processes, so he was putting forth the overriding message, unless and until something changes, this is the outcome. He has every hope that something would change and intervene to prevent this inevitable outcome. But I think he would stand behind his point—and I would stand behind his point—that if something doesn't change, a military option becomes the lesser of evils."[36]

Yet Hagee's own rhetoric over the previous year showed a bloodlust for military confrontation. Just two months after the release of *Jerusalem Countdown,* Hagee told the *Jerusalem Post,* "I would hope the United States would join Israel in a military preemptive strike to take out the nuclear capability of Iran for the salvation of Western civilization. It is as important to America as it is to Israel." Regarding diplomacy, Hagee added, "I don't believe that the Islamofascist mentality will ever respond favorably to diplomacy. Their agenda is the destruction of Israel and death to Jews and Christians." Hagee rejected sanctions as well, stating that "sanctions have never worked. Sanctions didn't stop North Korea. Sanctions didn't stop Cuba. Sanctions will not stop Iran." When asked whether Israel should be a part of a preemptive strike against Iran, Hagee maintained that "America could do it alone if they chose to."[37]

His fiery rhetoric continued through the summer of 2006 and

the Israel-Hezbollah war. Late in the summer, when McCain and Gingrich were using their inflammatory world war rhetoric, Hagee delivered a series of sermons arguing that World War III had begun. "Most Americans," said Hagee, "are simply not aware that the battle for Western civilization is engaged. If you compare world history from 1935 until 1939 we are reliving that era. In that era Hitler pledged to kill the Jews and the people of the free world were trying to come to grips with the rise of Hitler's dictatorship and the threat to democracy. Only Winston Churchill got it right!"[38]

Portraying himself as a contemporary Churchill, Hagee maintained that "we are in a very similar period! The people of America do not want to admit Islamo-Fascism is a threat to this nation. It is! They don't want to believe that Iran would use nuclear weapons against mighty America! They will!" And with a Bush-Cheney flourish, Hagee added, "America was attacked on 9/11 by Islamic fanatics who intend to destroy this nation. Few Americans ever stop to consider what losing this war will mean to every one of us." Hagee called on his fellow preachers: "It is time for every spiritual leader in this nation to shake ourselves out of this stupor called 'political correctness' and to clearly and forcefully address the fact . . . we are at war with Islamic fanatics who intend to destroy the United States of America and Israel."[39]

Hagee's annual Night to Honor Israel has included Tom DeLay, the disgraced former House majority leader, as keynote speaker as well as Senator John Cornyn (R-TX) and Benjamin Netanyahu, former prime minister of Israel. Like many Word of Faith enterprises, the event has blossomed into a franchise. In 2007, at least forty Nights to Honor Israel were held across the country, with Hagee in attendance, mostly at Word of Faith churches from coast to coast.

Republican officials and candidates are seeking Hagee's ear. John McCain met Hagee for a private tête-à-tête in San Antonio, emerging with a virtual endorsement of his presidential candidacy and a $1,000 contribution to his campaign.[40] McCain hired influential San

Antonio lobbyist Tom Loeffler as his campaign finance chair. Loeffler, who heads a law firm and a lobbying shop, counts Hagee's son-in-law, Nathan Ketterling, as an associate at his law firm and the government of Saudi Arabia as a client.[41] Loeffler has been a major GOP fund-raiser and was a Bush Super Ranger in 2004, meaning he bundled in excess of $300,000 in contributions for the campaign.[42] Presidential hopefuls Sam Brownback and Duncan Hunter spoke at Nights to Honor Israel in South Carolina and Virginia. When Hagee was in Washington to deliver a well-received speech at the American Israel Public Affairs Committee conference in March 2007, he met with House Republican Whip Roy Blunt and other members of the House Republican leadership. Gingrich also collaborated with Hagee, delivering the keynote address at CUFI's 2007 Washington Summit.[43]

"We're All Jewish!"

The fixation on everything Jewish can be seen at Word of Faith churches all over the country. Parsley has appropriated the shofar in the celebration of his "jubilee" fiftieth birthday. At the Gimenezes' church in Virginia Beach I met a woman in the parking lot who was teaching a man how to blow a shofar. She blows it, she told me, only when the Lord tells her to, but when she does, she can really feel the anointing flowing all over her. I met a white man there who was wearing a tallith over his dashiki and told me he was a follower of Parsley. Kenneth Copeland's ministry was selling the five books of the Torah, in Hebrew with English transliteration and translation. Copeland's staffers told me his wife, Gloria, uses them to prepare her preaching messages. Anne Gimenez wrote in her 1993 book, *Beyond Tradition*, that Easter is a pagan holiday and that her followers should celebrate Passover instead. I've seen numerous people at Word of Faith churches wearing stars of David, and I saw one woman wearing a T-shirt that read "Shabbat: Just Do It." One evangelist I met in Tulsa, when she discovered I was Jewish, said, "Well, we're all Jewish!" and then offered to help me walk with Jesus because that "changes everything."

Hagee is obsessed with stereotypes of Jews being wealthy and claims that it is Satan—who is blamed for questioning the wealth of Word of Faith televangelists—who invented anti-Semitism out of envy of Jewish wealth. During an appearance on Copeland's program, wearing a tallith, Hagee told his friend: "Abraham was very rich in cattle and gold and silver. . . . That's why Satan himself hates the Jewish people."[44] Of course, it's the *stereotype* that Jews are rich or control the banks or control the universe (somewhat like Hagee's Antichrist) that has fueled anti-Semitism through the centuries. But Hagee covets what he depicts as the Jews' supernatural blessing, wondering aloud why Jews are only 2.7 percent of the population yet represent 80 percent of Pulitzer Prize winners. The Jews, Hagee claims, the descendants of Abraham, understand how to confer supernatural blessings upon themselves with the precepts of Word of Faith. "Once spoken into existence, the blessing cannot be broken by another man. No one can take your blessing once it has been spoken into your life."[45]

FIVE

Miracle or Rip-off?

When you look at the Bible and you see how God
set up a structure for underwriting those people
who work in the church, which includes the pastor,
you'll find out if you step back and do the math,
you'd expect the pastor to be the highest paid
person around.

—Dale A. Allison Jr.

That's just horseshit.

—Ole Anthony

At a table of books, CDs, and DVDs of Kenneth Copeland's teachings and preachings for sale, a woman approaches with her young son, who is in a wheelchair. "Give me everything you have that's new on healing," she tells the two young women working the table, who look as though they've stepped out of a Talbots catalog. "DVDs," she specifies. Smiling at the bright-eyed, sandy-haired boy, the cheerful saleswomen start handing over DVDs to their eager customer and show the boy each one to make sure he hasn't already seen it.

As the mother is preparing to purchase the DVDs, she and Copeland's staffers start talking about his new jet, a $20 million Cessna Citation bought with donor funds. The jet transported Copeland to Norfolk for the Assembly 2007 conference in Virginia Beach, where Copeland preached and bragged about how his theology has conferred on him a "blessing" and made him rich and healthy. His employees and fans don't question the extravagant plane. It is a symbol of his success and manhood; being a pilot is part of his allure. One of the ministry staffers giggles and says, "It's very loud. When it takes off, we can hear it and we say, 'Oh, Kenneth must be going somewhere.'"

Copeland's ministry was reported to have purchased the $20 million plane in 2006, shortly after he and his wife pulled out of a multi-million-dollar investment in a company they had claimed would build affordable housing in Dallas and across the country. When the Copelands suddenly backed out of the venture, they left vendors and contractors with tens of thousands of dollars of unpaid bills. News reports indicated that the vendors had no recourse because the investment was structured as a limited partnership, and the Copelands were not responsible for any company debt. Even vendors who were only owed a few hundred dollars were left high and dry, one of them noting that Copeland's lunch expense was probably the equivalent of what she was owed.[1]

The plane takes off from a private airport at the Eagle Mountain International Church compound north of Fort Worth, a $22 million complex that also includes the church pastored by Copeland's daughter and son-in-law, Terri and George Pearsons. Copeland and his wife, Gloria, also live on the compound, on a twenty-four-acre plot of lakefront land in an eighteen-thousand-square-foot home, also owned by Eagle Mountain, according to Tarrant County public records. The entire complex, owned by the federally tax-exempt church, is also exempt from local property taxes.

The private jet has become the transportation mode of choice among many successful Word of Faith preachers, who use donor funds to finance a luxury most donors could never dream of affording, all in the name of preaching the gospel. You will be blessed, they promise, by financing their trips around the world; the "blessing" will come back to you in untold ways. Benny Hinn has begged his followers for a $1,000 seed so he could buy a Gulfstream G4SP, which he dubbed *Dove One*. Hinn claimed that the jet "is designed and destined to become one of the greatest ministry tools in the history of mass evangelism" as he promised his donors they would become "part of this historic miracle!"[2]

The miracle seems to be that people keep giving. Flight records reportedly show that the Copeland jet has taken detours during world evangelism tours to luxurious hotspots like Maui, Fiji, and Honolulu.[3] Copeland has even used one of his airplanes to fly into the private airstrip at the LaFonda Ranch in Brackettville, Texas, owned by Hagee, where Copeland and his son have hunted rare exotic game. Jakes's jet takes frequent detours to Puerto Vallarta, Mexico.[4]

Part of the "gospel" Copeland and his imitators preach is the claim of faith healing. The fact that he recycles the same hope repackaged in a new DVD box didn't stop the woman with the disabled son from grabbing up whatever "new" teachings were available. To those who continue to hold out hope of miracles, Copeland is anointed. As one Copeland follower told me, "He speaks prophetically, in other words, he speaks the word of God."

But for some people, Copeland's healing claims can have deadly consequences. Kristy Beach tells how her mother, Bonnie Parker, died of breast cancer in 2004, after spending nearly ten years—without her family's knowledge—waiting for Kenneth and Gloria Copeland's messages to heal her.[5] Beach is certain that Parker became entranced with the Copelands through television. She has calculated that her mother sent tens of thousands, possibly hundreds of thousands, of dollars in donations to the Copelands over a ten-year period in hope of a phenomenal healing of her cancer. Notes she left behind indicate that she was always worrying that she wasn't giving enough. After the untreated cancer had ravaged her mother's body, Beach discovered her mother's secret life, too late, in reams of notebooks in which her mother documented her faith in the Copelands' teachings and her hopes that her "seed" would result in her supernatural cure.

When she first discovered her mother's notebooks, filled with hopeful pleas, Beach was bewildered—and angry. Her mother's expenditure of money, resting on false hope, seemed endless. "She bought Powerball tickets and things that she put into her Bibles and her notebooks," said Beach. "If you'll look on those and see where it says Powerball numbers, . . . its got Kenneth and Gloria's name on it, for the numbers to win the Powerball that would ensure that she'd have enough money for the healing. . . . When I'd seen that, oh my God, it made me sick; it still makes me sick." When she found out that one of her young children had secretly helped her grandmother stuff envelopes with hundred-dollar bills to send the Copelands on a weekly basis, Beach wrote the Copeland ministry for an accounting of her mother's donations. In return, she got a form letter, asking her to "sow a seed."

Looking back, Beach recalled only a couple of occasions that gave clues into her mother's secret life. When Parker revealed her cancer to the family—too late for treatment—and Beach was taking care of her, she asked her mother why she had not sought medical care. According to Beach, her mother "simply said she had not sowed enough seed yet, but when she did she would be healed. I asked her what she meant by this. She said everything was going to be OK, nothing else. Seed, what does that mean, I had no idea." During that same period, Parker asked Beach to take her to a healing school in Texas. "I was furious," Beach wrote in her own personal account of her mother's tragedy, that "she would go to this school but not to see a doctor." Beach wondered, "Who taught this school, and what did they teach? Why was her belief in this place so strong? I knew so little about her life back then." To imagine what Parker was hoping for, Copeland's own words provide hints: "You must accept God's Word as final authority. What it says, it means. When the Word says you are healed, *you are healed*! It doesn't matter what your body says about it. If you will believe this and operate accordingly, then the covenant you have with God—His Word—will become the absolute truth in your situation, and your physical body will come into agreement with the Word."[6] Since her mother's death, Beach has spent countless hours researching Word of Faith teachings to understand what had so hypnotized her mother. "If only I knew then what I know now," she wrote in her anguished narrative.

Parker's desperation, hidden even from her own husband, is documented in the notebooks. "It's so sad," said Beach in a tearful interview, "because she's saying in there that she don't want to die and that over and over and over, please heal me, please heal me. Please heal me is just on one page, over and over and over and it's their saying that if you have enough faith you're going to get healed, but if you don't have enough faith you're not going to get healed. It's just sad. And it just breaks my heart every time I even think about it that she went through all that, that many years." Beach now knows that the Cessna Citation the ministry staffers laughed about as they sold more healing tapes to a little boy in a wheelchair was paid for with her mother's money—and her life.

God on the Move

The plane is an essential accessory for Copeland's imitators. On *Larry King Live* in August 2005, the CNN host asked Parsley, "Should a pastor have a large home? Should a pastor have a private airplane? Should a pastor have a limousine?" Parsley replied, "Larry, I do at least 150 nights a year away from my family. I believe in family, so our ministry, for about twenty years has owned one aircraft or another, to get me back and forth to those appointments." King retorted, "You got a calling from the Lord and you're flying in a private plane?" Parsley sanctimoniously responded, "Everything's relative. If I can reach more people that way than any other way with the good news of the Gospel of Jesus Christ, that he came to humanity to give them peace and purpose, then I think people are very supportive of that. I know the people that support our ministry have always been."[7]

In a photographic history of Parsley's life and church at World Harvest Church, Parsley boasts that over the years he has had four different planes that have shuttled him more than a million miles around the world, allegedly to preach the gospel. The current plane is dubbed *Shamgar VII*, which Parsley translates as "God on the move." (In the Bible, Shamgar was a judge who slaughtered six hundred invading Philistines with an ox goad.)

Yet Parsley, like Copeland, takes detours for pleasure on the plane that he finances with tax-exempt donor funds.[8] In April 2007 Parsley's plane was in Carlsbad, California, for more than a week. During that time, Parsley was scheduled to tape *Praise the Lord* at TBN's Atlanta studio to promote his upcoming Reformation Generation youth conference, but without explanation the network changed the guest lineup for the program. Also during the week that his plane was in California, he was supposed to speak at the Gimenezes' Assembly 2007, but God's spiritual general, instead of speaking to his fans about America's Christian heritage, remained in California. That Sunday, the plane flew to Las Vegas for a few hours and then back to California. About gambling, Parsley has said that in his experience as a pastor, "I have seen the devastating effects of gambling. When I think of gambling, I don't see dollar signs. I see greed, exploited families, domestic violence, increased crime, child abuse, hunger, homelessness, and even suicide."[9] On the Sunday his jet was in Las Vegas, Parsley spoke to his church via telephone.

The jet remained in California for two more days, with a four-hour side trip to Los Angeles, a twelve-minute flight that probably cost thousands of dollars. An operator answering the phone at Parsley's World Harvest Church said that Parsley was indeed in California but that he had no preaching engagements there. When asked what he was doing, she laughed and said, "I have no idea; they don't give me that information." Parsley refused to explain what his ministry's jet was doing in Las Vegas that weekend. He returned to Columbus only to turn the plane around for a twelve-day trip to Port

Saint Lucie, Florida, again with no official preaching engagements on his public itinerary.

Parsley has been repeatedly criticized for his extravagant lifestyle, his authoritarianism, and his preaching of the prosperity gospel, but none of it seems to shake the faith of his most devoted followers. Mike Johnston, a car salesman who has belonged to World Harvest since the 1980s, says that Parsley "deserves what he does get paid, I do not know what that is, but I'm sure it's a significant number." Johnston doesn't seem to think he has a right to question how much Parsley makes, because "that's between him and God, that's not between him and I. I'm not here to judge why he should live in a beautiful brick home or have nice vehicles or whatever. That's just because he's sacrificed and worked very hard to spread the Gospel. . . . Now, do people give a lot of money to that ministry? They sure do, they absolutely do."[10]

"Protection Racket Gospel"

Parsley further propagates his message through his World Harvest Church Ministerial Fellowship. Pastors under the fellowship's auspices—or in the fellowship's parlance, "covering"—launch their own churches where, like a franchise, they employ his message and techniques. Tim Wirth is a born-again Christian and musician who attended and played in a band at a Parsley "church plant," Steadfast Harvest Church, in Troy, Ohio, in the 1990s, and has also has performed at World Harvest Church. He is now a blogger who is critical of Word of Faith as "almost a religion that was developed out of Amway, because it would be like, you're just weak, you don't know that you're just one day from your blessing. It hasn't hit yet. Just like in Amway, they say, you may draw that circle for the next person who's going to propel you into millions. So it was always like, yeah, you don't have it yet, but . . . keep 'em following, keep 'em pumped up." The pastors in Parsley's fellowship, Wirth added, "are so wrapped up in the cult of personality, they want to be like Rod Parsley, . . . [they] mimicked his sermons. It's duplication, again, Amway, you know. . . . Doesn't matter that the process doesn't have to do with anything in the Bible."[11]

Wirth says his questioning of the Word of Faith message and his ultimate departure from the church after Jim Hughes declared bankruptcy didn't sit well with the church leadership. "When I left that church, Hughes was very angry with me because—it's almost like a protection racket gospel, is what I compare it to." Wirth explained, "If you leave that church, you're no longer under their covering. I said, well, you know, that's cool, I'm under God's covering. I mean, I'm saved, and God will take care of me and my family. Because at first I was unfamiliar with the term, so I thought, covering? What, do you have your deacons rolling by my house to make sure that nobody robs me or something? And he said, I just want you to know, you're no longer under this church's covering and protection. Quote unquote."[12] Hughes eventually left Ohio and started a new church in Atlanta, where he remains a member of Parsley's World Harvest Ministerial Fellowship.[13]

The covering is for sale. Parsley makes his money through aggressively seeking tithes and offerings in church, but also through the commodification of his brand of the gospel. Isaiah 54:17 says "no weapon formed against thee shall prosper," and for $25, Parsley will send you a "No Weapon" backpack, accessorized with dog tags, a water bottle, wristband, T-shirt, and a handbook. Whether he's pleading for an Easter-season "resurrection seed," or a $40 gift to become a Platinum Covenant Partner who will be "in a close, inner-circle relationship with me," Parsley has a seemingly bottomless bag of tricks to part parishioners from their money.

Parsley also specializes in tugging on the heartstrings, even if it means exploiting global humanitarian crises. Janice Fisher, who lives in Dallas, is a paraplegic and homebound. She saw Parsley making a pitch for saving Christians in Sudan and sent $40 for a kit that allegedly included a pot, tent, and other supplies. Fisher saw Parsley's plea when "I was just flipping the station. I had seen it before, because he puts it up all the time. And of course he had a woman on there who supposedly came from there [Sudan] and some other man who came from there, and they had a story about it, and it was just heartbreaking. And it was supposed to go to the Christians."[14] Parsley frequently uses his *Breakthrough* television program to plead for money for Sudan relief that he says his Bridge of Hope ministry performs, including relief efforts and redemption of Christian slaves kidnapped by Muslims. But when Fisher received an acknowledgment letter, "It said it [my donation] might be used for other projects that he had. That made me so mad."[15]

When Fisher received her credit card statement, it showed the charge was made to "WHC Event Sales, Columbus, Ohio." (WHC is the acronym for World Harvest Church.) Fisher finally had the charge removed after complaining to Parsley's ministry, but she now believes that "when he's advertising—and he's still doing it—when he's advertising on there that this is going to the Sudan relief or Darfur, . . . and then you get a letter saying it might go somewhere else, that's bait and switch."[16] Parsley refuses to document how much money his ministry has brought in for Sudan relief and how much actually gets sent to Sudan.[17]

As recently as late 2006, Parsley was soliciting money for Christian Sudanese slave redemption.[18] Yet the principal Christian relief organization involved in the redemption of slaves in Sudan, Christian Solidarity Worldwide (CSW), abandoned the practice in 2000 "after it was decided that the policy had achieved the desired aim of drawing greater international attention to the forgotten horrors that were occurring in southern Sudan," said Dr. Khataza Gondwe, a spokesperson for the group.[19] (Critics of the practice maintain that it actually encouraged the kidnappings, as the kidnappers realized they could be paid to continue to enslave people.) Dr. Gondwe added, "CSW has never worked with Rod Parsley, as we have not been not aware of his work, nor of his organisation, Bridge of Hope Ministry." Christian Solidarity International, the relief agency with whom Parsley claims to work, declined to comment about its affiliation. Another relief worker who had done work in Sudan for government agencies and nongovernmental organizations for years also had never heard of Parsley or his ministry.

Give Until It Hurts

Rick Ross, who operates an eponymous institute that tracks cults and controversial groups and movements, says that Word of Faith is a movement that preys upon people using an environment of peer pressure to validate the leader's "anointing" and "give until it hurts." Peer pressure, says Ross, creates an environment in which people fear questioning the pastor. "When you're in a mass of people, twenty thousand people, in some arena, and they're all going along with what the preacher claims, ... there's an enormous amount of peer pressure to agree, and these people certainly put themselves in a position of being seen as anointed and special and prophetic." Ross has worked with relatives of a former member of one of Kenneth Hagin's Rhema churches, in North Dakota. Members of the church raised "critical questions about the administration of the church, about the behavior of the pastors, and concerns about the influence that they wielded over people." People within the church who questioned the amount of money they were asked to give and the lack of transparency within the church were "labeled as rebellious, and even at times, under the influence of Satan, and that caused rifts in relationships and families and marriages. ... It isolated people."[20]

One former member of Hagee's church, fearful to talk on the record because Hagee is "really powerful" and has "got so much clout," described Hagee as "very angry" and "not approachable."[21] The former member, who attended Cornerstone for about ten years, recalled that she had been going to Cornerstone for six years before she actually met Hagee. "I said, 'Oh, Pastor Hagee, I'm finally getting to meet you after six years,' and he said, 'Oh, I've been back here every Sunday' and turned and walked off." Her husband is bipolar, and when they went to marriage counseling, the church "told him he was a loser and an infidel." The counselors encouraged the former congregant to leave her husband, but "thankfully, I prayed enough. . . . I began to see trouble, you know, I began to see things that wasn't right."[22]

About the tithe, the former Cornerstone member recalled, "That's a shame issue there if you don't tithe. . . . We've heard him say, . . . everybody who's got their tithing envelope, wave it in the air. So that's shame on you" if you don't tithe.[23] Yet Hagee, before he converted his nonprofit Global Evangelism Television into a church in 2004 (thus relieving him of the obligation to file a publicly available tax return), was known to be the highest-paid nonprofit executive in San Antonio, making nearly $1 million a year.[24] Now, because of the conversion, his salary remains a secret. In 2000 his John C. Hagee Royalty Trust, whose trustee is Hagee's brother-in-law Scott Farhart, spent $5.5 million on a ranch in Brackettville, Texas.[25] The property includes the Hagee-owned LaFonda Ranch, which has its own private airstrip, where Copeland landed his aircraft for a weekend of hunting rare exotic game.[26]

Another component of Hagee's ranch is a cattle-raising operation. For that project, Hagee formed a nonprofit—run only by himself—called the Texas Israel Agricultural Research Foundation, which he claims works on joint research endeavors with an Israeli university. Water consumption is highly regulated in the parched section of the state where the ranch is located, but San Antonio legislator Frank Corte introduced a bill that would have exempted Hagee's outfit from the state's water use laws. To move the bill, Hagee enlisted the services of one of San Antonio's most powerful lobbyists, David Earl.[27] Members of Hagee's church sent more than eighty nearly identical letters—some from the church's fax machine—to the Texas House of Representatives committee considering the bill, urging its passage. The letters argued that the bill would "protect Texas agricultural research projects that have entered into agreements to share information with Israeli organizations." The bill stalled in committee, and Hagee's lobbyists were forced to apply for permits from the local groundwater control board in Kinney County to pump water on the property.[28]

Other Hagee ventures operate through trusts and companies run by Farhart and involve prominent San Antonio businesspeople. These ventures include a failed investment in a proposed hotel in downtown San Antonio and a planned development near his church. In another venture, Hagee crossed a group of local businesspeople who sought to market their beauty products made from salt from the Dead Sea through Hagee's ministry. They charged in a 2006 lawsuit that they entered into the deal after Hagee billed himself "as someone that had a lot of political connections," making the group "aware of his rubbing shoulders with people influential in the Bush cabinet," according to the group's lawyer, Jesse Castillo. Castillo said that his clients claimed that Hagee backed out of the deal because the church was facing tax problems due to "a concern that they were mixing the business interests of the church with the business interests."[29]

The former congregant whose husband is bipolar said that even though she and her husband wrote a big check to the church after they sold their house and tithed close to 10 percent of their income, "We never prospered there." Most of the people she knew there were struggling financially, including some who were evicted from their apartments because they couldn't pay their rent. Hagee, she said, has a "very powerful hold, and you don't even realize it. . . . We were there ten years, and I knew something was wrong, but I couldn't figure out what it was." She even feared speaking to a reporter: "If I say too much about him, God's going to get me. . . . [Hagee's] got so much money and he's so powerful, he could take everything we have in a minute."[30]

Another former member told of tithing even when she had to borrow out of her 401(k) plan to make her mortgage payments. At one point, she said, "at Christmastime I didn't have gifts under my tree. Two small gifts for my kids, that was it. I was so broke, and I was tithing." At the time, she believed that tithing would result in her own blessing. Still another former member, a single mother divorced from an abusive husband, told of tithing out of her child support checks, even though she was living in an apartment with subsidized rent. Contrasting her small apartment with Hagee's home in an exclusive San Antonio subdivision and his multimillion-dollar ranch, she added, "I don't even have a house! My kids grew up on top of each other like sardines. . . . I just want a little house." She added, "I thought something was wrong with me. Why am I still [living like this]. I've given and given and given and tithed and tithed and tithed." But while attending Cornerstone, she, like the others, felt guilt and enormous pressure not to question Hagee or his doctrine, and that atmosphere was reinforced through multiple church services each week and mandatory meetings with smaller cell groups whose leaders were vetted on the basis of classes, tests, and the faithfulness of their tithing. As a result, the former member said, "I looked to Pastor Hagee as a god."[31]

The Highest-Paid Person Around

Parsley today refuses to answer questions about his affiliation with his former attorney, Dale Allison, who set up his authoritarian church structure. Allison still maintains that church members have no right to question how their tithes and offerings are used, insisting that there is no biblical or legal requirement for a church to disclose an audited financial statement. Contrary to the financial accountability standards adhered to by most nonprofits, including many churches, as well as the standards of the Evangelical Council for Financial Accountability, Allison declared in 2005 that "it's very simple. If you follow the biblical example of giving a tithe and offering, then that's a gift. If it's a gift, it's no longer yours, so your interest in it should disappear." All that is required of the giver, Allison says, is to "be obedient to the word of God in giving his tithe and offering, and [once] he's done that, all he has to do is look for the blessing that God bestows on him for his obedience. He doesn't have to ask the church to account for how they're spending the money." The Bible is Allison's reference point for his statement that the pastor should be the "highest-paid person around."[32]

But while he was making sure Parsley would be the highest-paid person around, Allison himself declared bankruptcy. Parsley has refused to say whether he knew in 1987 that Allison had declared bankruptcy, and if he knew, why he continued to use the lawyer's services for nearly another decade (Parsley himself teaches that poverty is evidence of a lack of faith in God). Allison's bankruptcy filings show that he viewed the proceeding as a game; in one filing, he listed a Lucifer Fallenangel at P.O. Box 666 as one of his creditors. According to the court order disbarring Allison, in the years preceding his bankruptcy, Allison and his preacher client Simmons created multiple phony companies, often using fake names. They used these companies to take out bank loans, incorporate businesses, and orchestrate a phony foreclosure on Allison's house. A person familiar with Allison's bankruptcy proceeding described a "vast and complex" scheme to deceive Allison's clients, some of whom were also members of Simmons's church, and to hide assets; the person described as the scheme as "very sordid and very rotten." But Allison got away with it. In 1992 he was discharged from bankruptcy without any money having been distributed to his creditors.

Shortly after his bankruptcy discharge, however, the Georgia State Bar opened an investigation of Allison. While the bar's three-year investigation of Allison was ongoing, Allison continued performing legal work for World Harvest Church and served on the church's compensation committee, which determined Parsley's salary and benefits. In its order disbarring Allison, the Georgia Supreme Court found that he had engaged in criminal activity, including using fictitious and forged names on loan applications and state corporate filings.[33]

IRS: The Beast

Mark Hanby, the evangelist promoted by Jakes and Pearson, serves on the board of Beyth Anowth Ministries, the nonprofit through which Allison offers consulting services to churches, as does Calvin Simmons. Allison set up the business structure for Hanby's ministry and serves on its board. The pair also attempted to launch a Christian television network in 2001, soliciting investors at churches, including Long's and Paulk's.

Allison and Hanby teach other pastors how to set up their tax-exempt organizations to maximize the spiritual authority of the pastor—and the pastor's compensation. In his book *You Have Not Many Fathers*, which Jakes endorsed, Hanby asserts that churches should be modeled "after His Word, not the principles of this world." According to one former Hanby associate who did not want his name used, Allison believed that "government is the beast of [the book of] Revelation. It's the evil one." (The beast, bearing the mark of the number 666, is the false prophet, or the Antichrist, the one who will usher in the one-world order during the period of false peace before the Second Coming of Christ.) That Allison believes the pastor's money belongs to God, and that the pastor should be exempt from taxes, was evident even in the words of one of his defenders, Samuel Brockway, a businessman who has also been involved in Allison's ventures, including Simmons's church. Brockway said of Allison in a 2005 interview that he is "a fine person; he's an upstanding fellow, who helps churches reorganize and protect themselves from the IRS" and "helps them with their business operations."[34]

According to the former Hanby associate, Allison set up "personal foundations for people," frequently in New York, in which pastors could place personal assets to avoid paying taxes or court judgments. "They [Allison and Hanby] don't have any moral qualms about doing this," he said. Allison also recommended paying church employees as contract laborers to avoid paying payroll taxes. The former associate said, "Dale would help hide things from the IRS; that was one of his big things. He and Mark had a thing about the IRS."[35]

Allison also set up nonprofits for Long and Paulk that brought scrutiny to both men. Paulk's nonprofit organization, Earl P. Paulk, Inc., set up by Allison under New York law, accepted contributions from other tax-exempt ministries rather than from individuals. That arrangement caused Paulk to pay a $260,000 tax assessment, said attorney Dennis Brewer, who has represented Paulk, although not in connection with that incident. According to Brewer, any contribution from one tax-exempt organization to another is taxable to the recipient, except when given as benevolence to the poverty-stricken.[36] The last tax return before the organization was disbanded in 2003 shows that it received $137,000 in donations and paid Paulk $128,000 in salary for twenty hours of work per week, in addition to the $274,000 salary he earned from his church. The 2002 tax return showed he was paid $151,000 from the nonprofit and $297,000 from the church.

Long appears to have had a similar setup. A 2005 *Atlanta Journal-Constitution* article reported that he was paid extravagant perks out of a nonprofit entity called Eddie Long Ministries, one of about twenty companies owned by the pastor. The perks, totaling $3.07 million, included $1 million in salary, use of a $1.4 million home on twenty acres, and a $350,000 luxury Bentley.[37] Although Long dismantled the organization in 2001, he transferred its $2.7 million in assets to his church. Corporate records show that Eddie Long Ministries was set up by Allison under New York law in late 1995, after the Georgia state bar had begun its investigation of his wrong-doing in connection with Calvin Simmons.[38]

Long defended his salary and perks, telling the newspaper, "We're not just a church, we're an international corporation. We're not just a bumbling bunch of preachers who can't talk and all we're doing is baptizing babies. I deal with the White House. I deal with Tony Blair. I deal with presidents around this world. I pastor a mul-timillion-dollar congregation. You've got to put me on a different scale than the little black preacher sitting over there that's supposed to be just getting by because the people are suffering."[39] In 2007, according to another article in the *Atlanta Journal-Constitution*, Long apparently was so busy that he preached a sermon with significant portions taken from the Web site Sermons.com, without attributing the words to their source. Long claimed a staff member wrote the sermon for him,[40] but the evangelist remained very nervous that the incident would tarnish his reputation.[41]

A Vision and Another Bankruptcy

In the late 1990s, Hanby and Allison attempted to launch a new television network, Kingdom Vision Network (KVN), which raised $8 million in a private offering before declaring bankruptcy in 2004. A former employee said that the money was spent on salaries, perks, studio space, and equipment, without a clear business plan. Long, Paulk, Pearson, and other lesser-known televangelists served on the board of directors; Long and Paulk helped sell the investment to their congregations.[42] Pearson, who continues to praise Hanby, said he knew nothing of Hanby's past personal or financial problems in the 1980s and '90s. Of the KVN venture, he said that "it was a great idea. He's a salesman. He sold us all on it. When he would stand in that pulpit and talk about it, people started going into their pockets and supporting it, because it was a brilliant idea." But Pearson admitted that although Hanby could raise the money, he could not

manage it.[43] Among the creditors seeking compensation in the bankruptcy proceeding was the IRS, which filed a claim that the company
had evaded over $200,000 in payroll taxes.[44]

Clayton Cline, a West Virginia businessman, sued Hanby and
Allison after KVN went bankrupt, claiming that they defrauded him
out of a million dollars. The case settled in early 2007.[45] Jay Ramirez
of the Kingdom Life Christian Church in Milford, Connecticut, said
he invested $200,000 of his own retirement savings in the venture,
"influenced by admiration for these people." In particular, Ramirez
said, "Hanby's credibility with many of us was very significant."
Ramirez recalled a meeting in Atlanta at which the investment
opportunity was presented, and he remembered Pearson and Paulk
and other "people that you trust and admire" in attendance, but
"probably the confidence in Dr. Hanby's reputation trumped all of
that."[46]

Although Ramirez did not feel he was "finagled" out of his
money, he was surprised to learn from me that Allison had been disbarred. "I was under the impression that he was an attorney," said
Ramirez. "He must have told me he was an attorney." A former employee of both KVN and Mark Hanby Ministries similarly was not
aware that Allison had been disbarred until 2003, and she found out
from another minister, not from Hanby or Allison.[47] In his biography
in KVN filings with the Securities and Exchange Commission,
Allison did not reveal that he had been disbarred, stating only that
he "spent over 25 years as a practicing attorney specializing in tax
exempt, nonprofit corporations until turning over all the legal aspects of Beyth Anowth Ministries to his son, Stephen, in 1997." He
claimed that he still consults to over seven hundred churches nationwide.[48] Ramirez didn't know about Hanby's or Allison's bank-
ruptcies, adding, "That would have been nice to know." Ramirez
added that Hanby could have been up front about his past problems
without jeopardizing his desire to invest. If Hanby had been, "the
level of his stature might have been able to overcome" that disclo-

sure. Still, despite losing his retirement savings, Ramirez felt "a lot of good" came from Hanby's teachings in his church.[49]

Touch Not Mine Anointed

Although Parsley has been accused for years of not using donor contributions for their promised purposes, gag orders and the IRS rules protecting churches from financial disclosure have enabled him to continue to operate in secret. And the authoritarian structure of his church—in which no one is supposed to question the "anointed one"—silences any critics within his church, and even within his own family. Three lawsuits were brought against Parsley in the 1990s, while Allison still represented him, including one by his aunt and another by his cousin. All were settled with gag orders that prevent the parties or their attorneys from discussing them, but publicly available records shed light on Parsley's authoritarian practices and his obsession with money.[50]

In 1992 a painting contractor who attended World Harvest Church, Lewis Bungard, alleged that Parsley choked him and that Parsley's father punched him after an argument over money owed him for painting Parsley's new home during which Bungard accused the pastor of deceiving his followers. Criminal charges against Parsley were dropped, Bungard claimed, after Parsley's assistants backed up the pastor's denial to police that he had assaulted Bungard. Parsley's father pleaded no contest to a reduced charge of disorderly conduct. According to court records, Bungard sued not only to recover the money he was owed under the contract but to establish a court-supervised trust to ensure that money Parsley had solicited to build a home for unwed mothers and a retirement home was used for those purposes. Bungard and his wife testified in depositions that based on Parsley's representations, they had donated about $7,000, sometimes in cash or by check. Because the case settled in secret, it is not publicly known whether such a trust was ever created.

After the incident at his house, and before Bungard filed his suit, Parsley condemned Bungard from his pulpit, accusing him of trying to extort money from the ministry. In the speech, Parsley drew battle lines between "two kingdoms" that are "antagonistic to one against the other." "If you ever expect this secular world, and this secular humanistic, self-promoted legal system, called the news media to ever tell the truth, you can forget that. Just forget it," said Parsley. "They have set themselves up higher than the courts of this land."[51] In sworn deposition testimony, Bungard said that other members of the church community ostracized him after he accused Parsley of wrongdoing.

Around the same time that Bungard filed his lawsuit, Parsley's aunt Naomil Endicott (his mother's sister) accused his father (her brother-in-law) of sexually harassing her while she was working at the church. When she filed her lawsuit, the church issued a press release that accused her of being a "disgruntled" family member who had engaged in a "pattern of manipulation . . . to obtain monies from the family and the church." That case settled in secret, too, after Endicott produced a tape recording she said proved the elder Parsley's harassment. In court papers, Endicott described an environment hostile to anyone questioning "self-serving, unethical, or inappropriate behavior" by Parsley and his parents. She also claimed that she was not paid for overtime work and that Allison counseled her to execute tax forms to elect to be exempted from Social Security coverage, which saved the church the cost of the FICA contribution. He did not explain that these decisions would reduce her Social Security retirement benefits. "These were presented as forms necessary to take advantage of a tax benefit for employees of non-profit corporations," she charged. Parsley has claimed that the church "makes all appropriate filings in accordance with all legal requirements," and Allison maintained that Endicott was a "minister" and therefore could opt out of Social Security benefits but that he never forced anyone to waive that right.

Parsley's cousin Dwayne Endicott sued Parsley in 1995, claiming that he was forced out of his job as a maintenance worker at the church after Parsley discovered that he had complained to a friend about the lack of overtime pay. In a sworn affidavit, Endicott testified that Parsley "yelled, screamed, and berated me for almost 10 minutes, stating that I was causing dissension and discord in the church." Parsley told him that he was "in rebellion against the church and against God and that I should 'stop lying and be a man.'" Endicott claimed that he was later called in for a staff meeting with Lester Sumrall—the Indiana evangelist Parsley credits as his mentor—who stated that "we should be careful what we say about 'God's anointed persons,'" meaning Parsley.[52]

Master Manipulator

The authoritarian pastor can wield power over congregants in other ways as well. Paulk is alleged to have taken his "spiritual authority" to the extreme when, former female congregants charge, he compelled them to have sex with him. Sexual misconduct charges against Paulk date back to the early 1960s, when he was removed from his Pentecostal denomination, the Church of God. Keeping that story under wraps, Paulk became pastor of a nondenominational church, Chapel Hill Harvester Church (later known as the Cathedral of the Holy Spirit) in Atlanta, which grew exponentially in the 1980s, when he preached a message of racial unity within God's kingdom in a city with a history of racial divisiveness. According to the *Atlanta Journal-Constitution*, during that period Paulk "claimed to have a revelation that Christians must establish God's kingdom on Earth. . . . A 'kingdom church,' Paulk explained in his 1984 book *Ultimate Kingdom*, is built on 'kingdom relationships' between individuals or within communities willing to submit to spiritual authority. At Chapel Hill Harvester, that authority was Earl Paulk."[53] At its peak the church had twelve thousand members.

Denise Weaver, who belonged to Paulk's church from 1986 through 2005, described Paulk as a "great orator" who was a "master at manipulating people, and it appeared to be real."[54] Weaver, who is black, was drawn by the message of racial harmony preached by the white pastor. She said the way he would minister to people at the altar made you think, "wow, this person . . . really cares and loves people." The love and racial unity in the church was how Paulk sold his "kingdom now" theology, that the kingdom is built on relationships, and, as Weaver put it, "everyone wants to be loved and accepted and cared for and so . . . he knew how to play that and he did." A lot of people bought into it, said Weaver, including other megachurch pastors that consider him their "spiritual father," among them, Eddie Long, who perpetuates the kingdom principles through his own teachings.

But underneath the uplifting message of love and unity was a dark secret that started to unravel in the 1990s, when six women in the church accused Paulk—one of George H. W. Bush's "thousand points of light"—of manipulating them into sex based on his theory of a "kingdom relationship": sex with the bishop (and in some cases members of his family or other pastors) was what God wanted for his kingdom. Instead of answering those charges, Paulk admitted to the thirty-year-old adulterous affair that led to his banishment from the Church of God in the early 1960s but said nothing about the current charges, despite nationwide television and print attention to the case.[55] Even in private conversations, Paulk refused to admit any impropriety.[56] Through the 1980s and 1990s and into the first years of the twenty-first century, Paulk continued to be exalted as a spiritual leader, as evidenced by visits by Jakes, Pearson, Hanby, and others and by offering spiritual guidance to Long, who went on to launch his own church, New Birth Missionary Baptist. "There is a network of these guys that support each other, look out for each other, know something is wrong with each other to some extent, and they cover for each other," said Johnny Enlow, who was a member of

Paulk's church from 1987 until 1992, and even became part of the church leadership.[57] Enlow wouldn't name names, but he said, "They threaten, through spiritual tones, people who would tell on them. And it's part of the overall effect, the effectiveness of them. Staying in power, and keeping people quiet, and keeping their own members believing them."

At the time Enlow considered the sexual abuse allegations "ridiculous rumors," but he left the church in 1992 for what he describes as "spiritual reasons." Those reasons included "a great lack of character, . . . a higher divorce rate among the young couples than . . . outside the church, . . . drug use and abortions, and all kinds of things that were [happening] at an alarming rate, not just equal to the unchurched but from what I could observe, even greater [than outside the church]." Enlow's chief concern "was that the cult of personality around Earl Paulk was so strong that there was more emphasis in serving and pleasing and listening to him than there was in serving and listening and pleasing God." After he left the church, "I became an enemy," said Enlow, "because I wasn't afraid of them [Paulk and the church leadership]." The six women all told Enlow their stories of sexual abuse, he said, which he came to believe were true. Paulk brought a slander lawsuit against Enlow and the women, and "we just heard through the grapevine that they [the Paulks] made a statement, if we're going down, we're going to take people down with us, and that their intention [was] to financially crush some of us, just by having to defend it legally." Paulk eventually dropped the suit, but he has continued to deny the sexual abuse charges.[58]

Enlow said he now knows ten women personally who say they were compelled to have sex with Paulk, allegations that Paulk continues to deny. "It wasn't like at gunpoint. . . . It was a pretty elaborate process [that] started[ed] with the cult of personality, with him being exalted to his high level and then twisting of Scriptures. . . . They would twist that . . . this is a ministry relationship, and marriage papers are just a piece of paper. God doesn't honor a piece of paper. He honors covenants of the heart, and things that strengthen relationships for the purposes of the kingdom."

Enlow described the church's "Madison Avenue ability to propagandize" the cult of personality around Paulk through "a constant flow of videos that would talk about the good things they were doing, and every word spoken positive to them or about them by anybody, that he was given George Bush Sr.'s one of the thousand points of light, and you have various government officials and leaders, a steady stream of them, coming in saying how awesome he was, and then spiritual leaders, leaders in all departments of life, coming in and saying what an awesome guy he is."[59] Much of that praise stemmed from Paulk's community outreach projects, which earned him plaudits from Republicans and Democrats alike. When President Bush summoned Paulk to *Air Force One* to bestow upon him one of his "thousand points of light," in February 1992, he remarked that he hoped Paulk's ministry would serve as a model for other faith-based organizations.[60] Enlow said that "there [were] probably legitimate things . . . but John Gotti did great things for his community. . . . Actually John Gotti probably did a whole lot more for his community."[61]

Membership in the Cathedral of the Holy Spirit declined after the 1992 firestorm, but Paulk built attendance back up, his program continued to be shown on TBN, and he continued to receive the support of fellow evangelists. Weaver recalled that Paulk and Hanby were "extremely close friends" and that Hanby's preaching was always "lifting him up, and building him up, to be this great man of God and father and all that," as the two shared the same ideas on spiritual authority and kingdom principles.[62] Even when a 2001 lawsuit brought by another church member, Jessica Battle, claimed that Paulk sexually abused her as a child,[63] a core of Paulk supporters remained with the church because, as Weaver recalled, "when you're in that atmosphere . . . they have a way of getting your attention off that kind of thing." Battle's mother and grandmother, said Weaver, even got up in front of the congregation and said the young woman was lying. Weaver recalled Hanby visiting to warn the congregation that coming against a "man of God" was "a really dangerous thing to do."[64] (Hanby sued his own stepdaughter in 2006, alleging that she had slandered him and damaged his ministry by discussing his messy divorce—his second—from her mother in blogs.)[65] Weaver said that because she never read the newspaper, including the *Journal-Constitution*, which covered the allegations, and she believed what she heard inside the church, she dismissed Battle's allegations as well as the other women's. "Of course his [Paulk's] thing was always, don't pay attention to the media, you already kind of had a thought process anyway that the media is always about trying to destroy the church."[66]

In 2003 Paulk settled the Battle case—under a gag order—with the financial help of one of his close friends in the ministry, Bobby Brewer, who lent him $400,000. Brewer says now that it wasn't until two years later that he found out that for fourteen years, Paulk was having sex with his wife, Mona. Only when the Brewers filed a lawsuit against Paulk in late 2005 and Mona Brewer told her story on CNN was there a mass exodus from the church.[67] That was when Weaver, a close friend of Mona Brewer's, finally left the church, after nearly twenty years of membership. Under the leadership of Paulk's nephew, the church has several hundred people who still attend services there.

Louis Levenson, who represented the Brewers in their lawsuit against Paulk, said Paulk was "authoritarian" and "imperious in his treatment of people, whether they brought him theological or management questions." If anyone did question him, they were "held up to scorn in front of the whole church," and anyone questioning his spiritual authority would be predicted to be "subject to some horrible fate."[68] Levenson said that Paulk required "absolute spiritual and theological obedience" and threatened women that they would lose his covering if they did not obey his "carnal commands." Paulk did not respond to an interview request, and one of Paulk's lawyers, Dennis Brewer (who is not related to Bobby or Mona Brewer), said a gag order prevented him from discussing the case.[69]

The Antichrist Hates It When You Drive a Nice Car

Money was a big component of Paulk's "spiritual authority" as well. According to Levenson, he "compelled obedience through tithing and gifting, including double-tithing." Weaver recalled that after Paulk built the enormous 8,800-seat Cathedral of the Holy Spirit, he demanded tithing and double-tithing "to the point where he believed if you didn't tithe, you were going to hell." Yet while Paulk claimed he needed the money to pay off the debt on the Cathedral, he and his family "lived pretty large," with a "huge home, . . . very nice, with huge fixings. . . . He drove a Lexus. Most of his family . . . had the same thing; they all had the big lavish homes and the nice cars and they went away on big trips and stuff."[70] When Paulk once pulled up to a small-town Hardee's in a limousine, a wide-eyed waitress asked what he did for a living. One of Paulk's companions joked, "If I tell you, I will have to kill you."[71] In an appearance by Hanby at Paulk's church in 1996, Hanby equated the ministry with the "high priests" of the Bible, and maintained that the tithe belongs to the ministry, which should not have to worry about "natural things."[72] "It's Antichrist, these spirits that hate it when you drive a nice car, look at you when you wear nice clothes," Hanby declared, to audience applause. In response to Hanby's dissertation on the proper "order" of the church, Paulk mused, "that is what prevents the provision of God from coming, if we are not in proper order."[73]

The circle of pastors around Paulk continues to protect him. Neither Jakes nor Long would comment on Paulk, but Pearson, while denouncing clergy sexual abuse as "absolutely appalling," called the women's charges that they were brainwashed "stupidity."

Both Paulk and the women were wrong, said Pearson, "and they ought to be on their knees before Sister Paulk, apologizing for seducing her husband, or having sex with her husband or committing adultery with him, as well as denouncing the preacher, and spreading it all over the media that this man was a human being being human."[74] Weaver questions why none of Paulk's peers speaks out against him, to say "this is absolutely wrong, and we will not tolerate it. To say nothing says everything to me."

Weaver says she now understands how Paulk's congregants fell under the spell of his "spiritual authority." "The reason I know this is because I was in there, and now that I'm out of there, I see how I was manipulated. You can't even see it a lot while you're there. It almost takes you to come out to really see what was really happening, to see how you're really being used and abused and not just the sexual abuse; it was abuse all through there. There was abuse even with me, I see it so clearly now. I really thought these people loved me, I really did! And now I know they didn't care anything about me."[75]

SIX

Praise the Almighty Dollar

If you could buy God, how much would you give?
—EDDIE L. LONG,
at TBN Praise-a-thon, April 10, 2007

In a forlorn section of DeKalb County, Georgia, prosperity seems elusive. But along highways lined with payday lenders, check-cashing stores, storefront DUI lawyers, run-down fast-food restaurants, and pawnshops sits one of TBN's television studios, from which the network broadcasts its prosperity message. Housed inside a pink brick building with plantation-like columns in the front and a bronze horse leaping out of the center of a fountain, the studio frequently serves as the set for TBN's *Praise the Lord* broadcasts. During the network's semiannual week-long Praise-a-thon, it is the home base for TBN's grande dame, Jan Crouch, and her stable of preachers, singers, and entertainers, who are dispatched to cajole the television audience into parting with its money in the name of Jesus. From 4:00 to 8:00 every evening of the Praise-a-thon, a live feed from this studio is broadcast all over the world, pleading with the audience to sow a seed in the network.

A security guard searches my bag and runs a metal detection wand along my body. I am ushered into the studio, which is much smaller than one might think from seeing it on television. I was told that the doors would open at 3:30, but when I arrive at about 3:00, the two hundred or so folding chairs set up in the studio are already more than half full. My usher, a middle-aged African American woman, has the demeanor of the church busybody, making it her business to put everyone else in their place. She even orders around the musical accompanist of Atlanta's best-known preacher, Eddie Long, while he waits for his boss, that night's star attraction. Long is not just a celebrity to the TBN audience but is known all over Atlanta, his billboards advertising his regular church service as well as his recent Easter extravaganza at the seventy-thousand-seat Georgia Dome. The usher insists the accompanist just wait in the audience. Long will call for me, persists the accompanist, not wanting to be in the wrong place when summoned. "Oh, I know he will," replies the usher. "I know Bishop. I've been a member for fifteen years." And with that, she exercises her own tiny authority over the musician who helps create the drama around Long's "anointed" preaching.

A sense of anticipation builds for a celebrity preacher. But in this small space it is quite obvious that you are being watched. The ushers make sure the crowd is enthusiastic but not speaking in tongues too loudly. Security guards, dressed in street clothes and equipped with secret service–type earpieces, flank the stage and encircle Jan as soon as she moves off it. The producer directs the audience to watch the camera with the long arm—that's the one that pans the studio audience for the benefit of those watching at home. Look for the camera, look happy, and don't leave your seat when it is looking at you.

I chat briefly with the women sitting next to me, but as usual it's pretty loud, with the ubiquitous Crabb Family warming up for their performance. I ask Cheryl, who appears to be about thirty, why she came tonight. She shrugs. She says she saw the Praise-a-thon on television the night before and saw the crawler advertising the celebrities who would be in attendance. "Hey, I like those people," she says she thought to herself. She points out the Honey Baked Ham boxed lunch under my seat. She and her companion, Shirley, seem pleased with the free meal. I've just finished lunch, but I take out the bottled water. Soon a young boy is seated next to me, but he puts his face deep in a Hardy Boys mystery.

Most of the audience, probably upward of 80 percent, is black. Many of them do not look as though they are prospering. Others are well dressed and well coifed, and a few women look as if they've just had their hair and nails done. Some older women are even dressed in their Sunday best on this Tuesday, church hat and all. The audience knows the words to all the songs and sings along as the Crabb Family does a sound check with "I Am a Friend of God."

The set is, like all TBN paraphernalia, a chintzy attempt at regality. On television it looks like a tawdry, pathetic attempt to re-create Versailles, but in person it looks even cheaper, a wall of fake bookcases and staircases to nowhere, where kitschy bronze cherubs recline atop moldings, Jesus appears in stained glass that looks plastic, and even the foliage isn't real. It is a monument to TBN, where wealth is held up as the ultimate goal, no matter how illusory it is. Just before the broadcast goes live, a TBN employee steps onto the stage to remind the crowd that "this [the studio] is all yours. Bet you didn't know you were so rich!" Meanwhile, the usher has detected three seats in the two front rows that have not been claimed by people who had reserved them. She plucks me and two other solitary souls out of our seats in the back for a second-row vantage point. A young African American woman sits next to me and introduces herself as Lucretia.

Just before the cameras go live, Jan takes the stage to prime the audience. I've only seen her on television, where she strikes the pose of a demure, nearly dim-witted Southern belle, for many years wearing billowy antebellum dresses along with her trademark tower of a wig, blonde tinged with pink. Now, although her wig is the same, she wears a long, shimmering pink A-line skirt and a black crew neck sweater. She's so casual in the studio that she frequently slips out of her sandals during the taping and stands in her stocking feet. A contemporary and old friend of Tammy Faye Bakker's, Crouch employs the same runny mascara formula as a ploy for television donations.

In front of the audience—but not the camera—Jan is no shrinking violet. Gone is the high-pitched voice, the obsequious pandering to the male preachers, the blithering girl talk with the females. Before the cameras are turned on, Jan Crouch commands the room, her voice full not of helium but of authority. And her authority is based on a Jesus who healed her, the Jesus who made her rich. You do not doubt this voice. Jan had colon cancer. Now it is gone. "No radiation, no chemo, just Jesus!" she beams to the audience, which murmurs its gratitude, some people shouting out their praise. "Bless her," says Lucretia, as if speaking of a beloved friend. "He went to hell for us," Jan continues, "because he didn't want to go to heaven without us." But this is not just about Jan's miraculous healing— medically undocumented, of course—it's also about money. "The gift of the anointing for prosperity is flowing on this Praise-a-thon," she proclaims. Then, in a disingenuous turn that is to become a theme for the evening, she adds, "the Praise-a-thon is not about TBN. It's about you."

Passover Offering

As with most Praise-a-thons, the main event—tonight, Eddie Long— is preceded by a lesser-known act. Long's warm-up is Steve Munsey, an Indiana pastor who just one month earlier hosted a CUFI-sponsored Night to Honor Israel at his megachurch. The following month Munsey would host Jakes on his book tour for *Reposition Yourself.* Munsey has made his own contribution to bringing Judaica into the Word of Faith movement, which he is peddling tonight. Munsey, a middle-aged man (an "empty suit," as described to me later by someone disenchanted with the movement) with a flop of a hairpiece that looks like straw, is imploring the audience not just to make a donation but to make a "Passover offering." Seven is a bibli-cally significant number, the number of completion and perfection, and in this spring of 2007 the Praise-a-thon began on Easter Sunday, the seventh day of Passover. If you make the Passover offering,

Munsey claims, God will give you seven blessings: God will dispatch an angel to lead miracles; rid you of your enemies; bless you with prosperity; heal you; give you longevity; give you an inheritance you knew nothing about; and give you back everything the devil has stolen from you. In other words, these are the ways in which the TBN Praise-a-thon is about you and not about Paul and Jan Crouch or Steve Munsey or Benny Hinn or Eddie Long or anybody else making more money. Instead, if you give, you will be blessed in miraculous ways.

Passover has nothing to do with money, but in Munsey's hands it is about little else. Gone is the biblical story of freedom from slavery, the journey through the desert with only the unleavened bread, or the parting of the Red Sea. Instead, a donation to TBN is like the blood Jews placed on the doors of their homes so that God would "pass over" and spare their first-born sons from death. Lucretia, the woman sitting next to me, grabs my arm. "Jesus was the Passover offering," she says. "His blood." Munsey is getting more and more animated while he preaches; the audience also is animated – almost agitated – over the possibility of the blessings. Munsey takes off running up the fake stairs on the set, but they don't go anywhere. "Oh!" he exclaims, surprised. "This is a dead end!" There is some uncomfortable laughter; it's hard to imagine anyone not questioning Munsey's brainpower in thinking the stairs went somewhere. Anyone in the room can see the stairs on the set are pretend, but Munsey was clearly hoping they led somewhere from which he could make a dramatic reentry onto the stage. Instead, he trots back down and resumes preaching, undeterred.

Munsey continues to implore the audience to part with its money. "God said, don't come empty-handed," he warns. In other words, give. The audience is shouting out praise, and people are filling out their envelopes. This seems far-fetched on television, but in person – just like at Parsley's healing service – many people are having genuine spiritual experiences. Munsey is working them up, and they are being milked for their money while in a euphoric state. Suggested donation for the Passover offering: $70 a month for ten months. Phone it in, and tell the operator it's the Passover offering, and "prosperity is going to come into your life, . . . and everything that has been stolen from you will be given back."

In TBN's world, God is not compassionate to the poor, only to the faithful, and their faithfulness is measured by their offering. It doesn't matter if the audience might need their money for the rent, for medicine, for food. Munsey says—to nods and murmurs of affirmation—that God is not merciful to the needy. "God is not moved by need," he insists. "If he was, there wouldn't be any poverty. What moves God is your faith," as evidenced by your donation to TBN. If you're poor and make the Passover offering anyway, Munsey promises, God will dispatch an angel to give your boss a nightmare in the middle of the night that will make him give you a raise. "God takes your offering and magnifies it in the devil's face."

The Passover offering opens up sensational, awe-inspiring occurrences, wonders and miracles, which the revelation knowledge of a Word of Faith believer tells them can really happen. Munsey regales the crowd with a story of a woman in his church who gave the Passover offering. Her husband later needed a kidney transplant. She agreed to donate one of hers, and when the doctors opened her up, it turned out she had three kidneys. "You can speak it into existence," says Munsey. "Life and death is on our tongue." People are walking up to the stage and placing their offering envelopes on it. "TBN is an altar," says Munsey, as if people are making offerings in a biblical temple. "And when you give on this altar, God will meet you there, bless you there, give you my name there."

Jan stands to ratify Munsey's spurious claims. Six weeks ago, she says, she got a report from the doctor that there was "something in that area"—she waves her hands vaguely around her abdomen, once again playing the jejune little belle who can't be bothered with mastering all that medical jargon—and couldn't rule out that her cancer had not returned. Two weeks ago, she asserts, she had laparoscopic surgery, then full-fledged surgery, during which doctors took nine biopsies. No cancer was found, she says. But something happened to her heart during the surgery, and she would have to have an echo-stress test, something she says Paul had and was very terrible. While lying in a hospital bed awaiting the test on her heart, she watched Munsey preach on Paula White's program about the Passover offering, and she was moved to make a $7,000 offering to Paula White's ministry. Miraculously, her heart was healed.

With the audience worked up by the possibility of seven blessings, devils rebuked, bosses scared out of their wits, healed hearts, and self-reproducing kidneys, Jan introduces Eddie Long as an agent of God. Calling him "one of the greatest prophets of our generation," Jan says that "every time I see him, I just want to bow down." When Long—wearing a custom-made, five-button, apricot-colored suit, a chunky gold watch, gold bracelet, and oversized rings—takes the stage, this great prophet not only endorses Munsey's teaching but creates a sense of urgency that if you don't follow it—and now—you might be missing a glorious opportunity. Turning to Munsey, Long tells him, "I believe everything you just spoke." To the audience, he says, "Every time I hear him, he takes me to school, because of the wealth of anointing, and words and secrets, . . . secrets that God releases in the spirit for those who are hungry to grab." Munsey and TBN reveal secrets to you. Those secrets tell you of miracles that can be yours if you seize them with your dollars.

For a full ninety minutes, Long preys on that sense of urgency. The pitch, depth, and volume of his gravely voice rise and fall. His accompanist (restored to his rightful place at the electric keyboard), pounds out notes of drama, of mystery, and of redemption, his fingers dancing over the keys to both create and amplify the mood. Long is a crafty choreographer. Almost like the supposed limited-time offer of an infomercial, Long maintains a carpe diem—lest the opportunity pass you by—atmosphere in the room. "This is not just a regular telethon. . . . This is a moment in time. We are not just raising money. We are raising the Holy Ghost to rule and reign over the earth. . . . We can either shoot up and subdue nations, or God will disqualify us and wait for another generation."

For Long, the telethon presents just another opportunity to preach on his kingdom theology, in which he merges old-fashioned dominionism—the right of Christians to take control over the earth—with a very contemporary form of individualistic, self-centered ambition achieved through righteous militarism. Long has moved beyond name it and claim it. Long is into *possessing* it—*it* being not just the earth but the earthly things on it, the airwaves, the realm of political discourse. "We are not just raising money for now, we are raising the Holy Ghost to rule and reign on Earth now!"

Part CEO, part self-help guru, and part battle commander, Long fancies himself the omniscient revealer of secrets to the dissatisfied and aimless, a leader of the lost into a battle with the devil over souls and property. Long, in his part as the CEO, the successful black role model, shouts, "God is using the TBN PA system, and he's blowing a wake-up call!" Citing Deuteronomy 1:6, Long exhorts his listeners to "go in and possess it." ("It," in Deuteronomy, is the whole of Israel, Lebanon, and the Euphrates River Valley.) Homing in on a mostly black and largely female audience—some of whom are old enough to have lived through segregation, and all of whom still face a struggle with economic inequality—Long implies that they haven't been brave enough to possess "it." Here, "it" means turning over their cash to TBN so they reap the abundance that is sure to follow. But the audience affirms the multimillionaire televangelist's cultural reference, implying that they have been complicit in keeping themselves down—by not reaching out for prosperity by giving money to TBN. "We know how to live off crumbs, we know how to take a ham hock and find some green stuff in the field and call it greens. Do you know how to eat steak? Do you know what to do with abundance?"

Long the self-help guru tells the audience they should pledge

money because "you have stayed too long in the present circumstances," but you're now "on another journey . . . out of the ordinary . . . away from your past!" The audience is shouting "yes, yes!"
and people are crying praise and speaking in tongues as Long tells
them that God is "disconnecting you from failure. . . . Just open up
your mouth and say words. . . . After I finish, where you were, you
won't be anymore. There's a shift in the house!" Long the CEO kicks
in with a little insider tip: "This [TBN] is God's secret announcement
place. . . . If you're waiting on another telethon, you'll miss God."
Lucretia, sitting next to me, shouts out, "Say it, Bishop!"

Long the general in battle compares the telethon to a "rally call
for the nations." Putting God's words in his own mouth, he says, "I'm
calling my people now. . . . If you're a king, bring your glory. . . . I'm
bringing my troops, . . . my resources." With another insider tip, and
the crowd beyond rapturous, Long adds, "I'm about to drop a secret. . . . This is no gimmick or nothing. If you get this, you'll never
beg, you'll never be in want, you'll never lack." The secret, though, is
self-enrichment masquerading as a military budget. God needs
money for spiritual warfare, Long warns, suggesting that only the
righteous will part with their cash. "President Bush is having a battle
with getting more funds for the military," says Long, but "God didn't
have a chapter on needing funds, but he has to have funds, he has to
have folks who are righteous enough to take what the wicked laid
up!" The Pentecostal imperative to take on the devil has now blossomed into full-fledged fund-raising scheme, homing in on prospec-
tive donors as they are in full experience of their charismatic gifts.
Long the militarist has just called them into battle. Now Long the
capitalist is about to tell them why.

"Rise up, claim your property," he shouts. "You have no authority when you have no property," he adds, noting that the first thing
God gave Adam and Eve was property—and not just any old property, the utopia of Eden. And the battle that will make that happen
will be waged from the studios of TBN. Long exhorts the crowd,

"This place is to serve as the spiritual Pentagon, Paul and Jan will call for the generals, and they shall come and give orders and direction to the people of God around the world!" Shouts of hallelujah and glossolalia create a cacophony that almost drowns out Long's words. "Touch not my anointing and do my prophets no harm!" Long barks the familiar refrain, before issuing orders of anointing to the audience. "Now is the time for the saints of the most high to rise up, to rise up, to rise up, and possess the kingdom. . . . You must enlist!"

Enlistment is the equivalent of a donation to TBN, and enlistees "will feel the release of the Holy Ghost." But it's not just about keeping TBN on the air. "We are not just sowing into airtime, we are not just sowing into satellites." It's about a "shift," terminology Parsley also often employs when speaking of "paradigm shifts" that will lead to a national revival. Seeing the audience in full Pentecostal mode and, echoing suggestions made by Crouch and Munsey that the rest of the world will dismiss them because Pentecostalism is seen as strange or silly, Long tells the ecstatic crowd that they are little gods: "Even though they are telling you you have lost your mind, tell them you have the mind of Christ. . . . You're not just seeing my physical body, but you're witnessing the spirit of God!" As the crowd speaks more loudly in tongues, Long shouts, "You are not trash, you are not junk. . . . You know it's your day!"

Munsey stands to buttress Long. "Thank God we have a network that's not ashamed of the Holy Ghost," he says, repeating the canard that criticisms of the network are made by bigoted anti-Christians who do not understand the charismatic gifts. Emphasizing that God is "the only one who can lift you out of poverty," Munsey returns again to the Passover offering and seeks to explain why Christians have not been making it for the past 1,700 years. Constantine, claims Munsey, changed the Hebrew calendar to the Gregorian calendar because he was intimidated by the wealth of Christians who made the Passover offering. It was Constantine, he maintains, who made

Christians celebrate Easter instead of Passover and then made Christians take a vow of poverty. "That is why the Antichrist spirit is in the pulpit," Munsey says, slamming the non–Word of Faith church. "That's why God raised up this network, so you can be blessed." Call and pledge, he urges the television audience. "We cannot present your offering unless you call. . . . The way you get out of your situation is you give yourself out." People are kneeling at the "altar"–the TBN studio stage–and there is praying and shouting and more speaking in tongues.

The frenzy that Munsey creates at the altar is the close of the television broadcast, but there is no decompression afterward. As soon as the cameras are turned off, the ushers begin shepherding people out of the studio–no time for fellowship or even a casual conversation. The doors in the back of the studio are opened, and we are all herded down a side hallway instead of the main lobby and escorted out side doors, where five church buses are lined up to take people home. Almost everyone who was inside boards a bus. Lucretia, who noticed that I did not make my Passover offering, wants to make sure I know it's not just about the money. She cites Romans 12:1 to me, that giving is also about the mind, body, and spirit.

Lucretia is a four year member of Long's church. She moved to Atlanta from California to start over after a divorce. She calls Long "a wealth of ambition," someone who "pushes you into obedience. It's all about obedience." I'm about to ask her how, but she volunteers that she obeyed God to come here tonight. She starts her work as a nurse at 9:00 p.m. and easily could have watched this on television. But God told her to come, and she obeyed. She can see I have more questions, but she backs away and says good night.

America's Most-Watched Faith Channel

Although TBN is the TV face of Christian preaching and offers up televangelists as the anointed teachers of the word, Christian critics have not only rejected its Word of Faith teachings but have called on donors to stop giving their money. In the spring of 2004, the Christian watchdog organization Ministry Watch issued a donor alert entitled "Trinity Broadcasting Network's Coffers Are Overflowing with Cash!"[1] Ministry Watch is run by former Templeton Investments executive Rusty Leonard, whose conservative credentials could not be better evidenced than by his membership in the influential Council for National Policy. The organization analyzed the publicly available tax returns of the network and found that it had cash and short- and long-term investments totaling about $280 million and a five-year profit of $285 million. Noting that the Crouches earned a combined $764,000 salary for 2002, Ministry Watch decried the "shockingly little" amount the network spent on its charitable programs. "This huge cash stockpile should be spent on their charitable purpose and not built ever higher each year. Yet, TBN continues to ask donors for more money without disclosing how much they already have."[2]

Just a few months later, the *Los Angeles Times* published a three-part exposé of the inner workings of TBN, including not only the lavish lifestyle of the Crouch family, with its mansions, luxury cars, and private airplane, but also evidence that Paul Crouch had paid $425,000 to his former chauffeur, Lonnie Ford, to settle a 1998 lawsuit in which Ford alleged he had to have sex with Crouch to keep his job. Ford, who had been in and out of jail on drug charges and one sex offense arising out of an encounter with a seventeen-year-old, had struggled for years with addiction and met Crouch while living at a TBN-owned drug treatment facility in Colleyville, Texas. A news investigation in 2004 by the Dallas affiliate of the Fox network reported that the facility was not licensed as a drug treatment facility but that TBN had sought on-air donations—often with tear-jerking pleas from Jan—to fund the center. TBN also settled a lawsuit filed by a teenager who claimed one of the treatment counselors gave out cocaine in exchange for sex.[3] Ford, who also sought treatment at the center, went on to work as Crouch's chauffeur, and the network gave him a rent-free house and even paid off some of his debts. Ford said that he first had sex with Crouch at a TBN-owned cabin.[4]

In 2003, Ford went to TBN's Costa Mesa studio and demanded $10 million in exchange for keeping a manuscript he had written about his experiences with Crouch a secret. TBN took him to arbitration to enforce the gag order that was part of the settlement of his 1998 lawsuit. Ford lost the arbitration and was still subject to the gag order when the *Los Angeles Times* published his allegations in September 2004. Based on investigations by the Trinity Foundation, the *Los Angeles Times* reported evidence that people close to Paul Crouch were distressed about his homosexuality. Benny Hinn's former bodyguard, Mario Licciardello, testified in a deposition in an unrelated case that he was present in 1998 when Hinn told a group of associates that Crouch had had an affair with his chauffeur but that his excuse was that he was drunk at the time. (Licciardello died in 2000. Six other witnesses told the *Los Angeles Times* that Hinn said no such thing, but one, an ordained minister, said he did.) The Trinity Foundation also recovered documents from the trash of Dennis Brewer, one of TBN's Texas attorneys, who wrote to other TBN lawyers that "I am absolutely amazed that Lonnie hasn't gone to Penthouse or Dianne [sic] Sawyer with his manuscript, notwithstanding the [judge's] injunction." Brewer also noted that Matt Crouch, Paul Crouch's younger son, upon learning of his father's settlement payout for Ford's 1998 lawsuit, told Brewer's law partner that "I am devastated; I am confronted with having to face the fact that my father is a homosexual." (The younger Crouch and Brewer's law partner, David Middlebrook, denied that such a conversation took place.)[5]

Crouch denied the allegations, and the network took the newspaper to court to prevent it from publishing the story. After the *Los Angeles Times* piece appeared, Crouch called the story "crap" and a "pack of lies right out of the pit of hell" on the air, and TBN cancelled that fall's Praise-a-thon. Another TBN lawyer, John Casoria, who is also the Crouches' nephew, told the Dallas Fox network affiliate that Ole Anthony of the Trinity Foundation "is not a credible source" and that the *Los Angeles Times* is a "left-wing and anti-Christian newspaper." Among the people coming to Crouch's defense was Bush adviser Doug Wead.

The other parts of the *Los Angeles Times* series examined the Ministry Watch concern that "questions regarding an extravagant lifestyle for [the Crouches] remain unanswered." In addition to their salaries paid from the nonprofit—as well as salaries to family members—the Crouches travel in a $7.2 million jet owned by the network, drive luxury cars, and charge extravagant dinners and antiques (beloved by Jan Crouch) to network credit cards. Three family members control the board of directors. Thirty network-owned homes, including several mansions, are available for their use in five states. The series also revealed that former employees knew Paul and Jan not as the happily married, devout grandparents they project on television but as a couple that "lead separate lives and rarely stay under the same roof."[6]

In the wake of the *Los Angeles Times* reports, Ministry Watch called for the establishment of an independent commission to take over governance of TBN. The *Los Angeles Times* series, together with the organization's concerns over the network's "dubious 'prosperity theology'" compelled the watchdog group to call for an independent investigation of the network and a full disclosure of its financial statement "to raise the theological, financial, management, and governance integrity of TBN to a level equivalent to those of most other major Christian ministries." But nothing of the sort happened, and TBN only lashed out at the *Los Angeles Times*. As Ministry Watch observed, TBN's press release "demonstrated an attitude of arrogance

[and] lacked the humility one might expect from a Christian organization. This should be of grave concern to Christians because nonbelievers following this story may develop false lifelong impressions about Jesus Christ based on TBN's aggressive response, which was more typical of political campaign rhetoric given the heavy use of character assassination as well as dubious representations of the truth."[7]

While the *Los Angeles Times* was breaking the story about Crouch's alleged homosexual affair, Rod Parsley was campaigning for Ohio's gay marriage ban, and Eddie Long was campaigning for Georgia's. Both men condemned homosexuality as irredeemable sin. More than a dozen other states had gay marriage bans on the ballot that fall, and the Republicans were aiming to turn out voters motivated by homophobia who would vote for Bush. Yet the revelations about Crouch's homosexuality did nothing to tarnish the reputation of TBN, or of the personalities like Parsley and Long and Hagee who regularly damned gay people in public and on TBN's airwaves.

The TBN crowd's protection of Crouch had more to do with dollars than damnation, however. About the *Los Angeles Times* piece, Carlton Pearson said:

> They [the other televangelists] didn't believe it. Because it
> was not ever adjudicated, it never came to full peak, it was just
> the secular liberal media—that's the way they all think of it—
> coming to attack a man of God and tear up our twenty four-
> hour Christian television. It's an anti-Christ spirit trying to take
> Christianity down, and we're not going to stand for it.

As a result, they closed ranks around Crouch:

> We protected Paul—I say we, the preachers and everybody—
> because I fall if Paul falls, the network goes down and impli-
> cates every other person. So people would cover for Paul and
> the network because that is how they get their money. They
> preach on that network. Of course they would say that's how

we reach the world with the Gospel—of course you understand
that part. But these guys, if we don't convince the world that
they're going to hell, and convince Christians to help us save
this world from going to hell, we don't have a ministry. So we
need to believe in hell . . . and believe that everybody who
doesn't accept our message or doesn't hear our message is
going there. And of course we're all too busy raising our
families, having our jobs, we all can't be on the road and go
to Africa and Asia and India to save the heathens. So we have
to pay the Benny Hinns and the Billy Grahams and the Paul
Crouches to get the message out. That's why they can raise 30,
40, 50, 60 million dollars on those telethons every time. . . .
TBN is the largest television network on the planet. And
through it, we all appease our guilt because we're reaching the
world with the Gospel of Jesus Christ. We're saving the world,
through Paul and Jan, they're our little dolls. . . . [Crouch] does
telethons to raise money, but all those preachers on there,
everybody has a book, a tape, a conference, a phone number
for you to call, what they want is your name and address, of
course, so they can send you letters saying help me to save the
world. Jesus is coming back the day after tomorrow, we don't
have much time, you need to give me everything you have, as
much as you can. And the people do it.[8]

Pearson knows how feared homosexuality is among neo-Pentecostals,
who inherited the strict Puritanism of their Pentecostal ancestors. He
attended Oral Roberts University with Ted Haggard and said that
Roberts's son, who committed suicide in 1982, was gay and that
Roberts kicked out gay members of the World Action Singers. But
because Crouch represents their money pipeline, the prosperity
preachers looked the other way. And while everyone was looking the
other way, the Republicans were looking to the preachers to rally the
faithful against the sin of homosexuality.

Three years after the *Los Angeles Times* reports, when Rusty
Leonard was profiled on the ABC program *20/20*, TBN again sought
angrily to discredit Ministry Watch. Although much of the informa-

tion ABC reported, such as finances disclosed on TBN's most recent (2004) tax return, was publicly available, TBN called the broadcast a "hit piece against Christian ministries."[9] TBN attacked ABC's use of Leonard as a source "who has a longstanding practice of attacking ministries who are not in agreement with his brand of theology to insinuate—not substantiate—that many Christian ministries might not be spending their donations properly." Crouch claimed that TBN's finances were completely transparent, but after TBN responded to the ABC piece, Ministry Watch downgraded TBN's "transparency grade" from a C to an F. (Ministry Watch similarly gives most Word of Faith ministries, including Jakes's, Parsley's, Copeland's, and Hagee's, an F for transparency.) Noting that TBN had $343 million in cash and short-term investments and another $53 million in long-term investments, Ministry Watch countered that "TBN's response was an attempt to divert TBN donors' attention away from the truth."[10]

TBN's enablers, like Long and Parsley, with their own history of antigay activism, have never addressed the claims of Paul Crouch's homosexuality. Instead, during the Praise-a-thon, Long fawned over the Crouches and repeatedly referred to the network as a "good work." He even took up arms against the murkily defined forces that are out to get TBN. During his appearance, Long protested that "the church has been begging too long. The church has been sick too long. The church has been in debt too long." But that, according to Long, can be fixed with viewer donations. The more serious problem, Long suggested, is one his viewers can't control. The real problem, he says, is that "the church has been ordered by government too long. . . . They're trying to shut us up. What's wrong with the name of Jesus? They're trying to shut us up."[11]

Terrorists, Jesus, and Hollywood

TBN uses its tax-exempt status to get free advertising and promotion for its for-profit movie production company, Gener8Xion Entertainment. Run by Matt Crouch and his wife, Laurie, the publicly traded company has received infusions of nearly $50 million in cash from the nonprofit to support its moneymaking ventures. Despite the free cash and advertising, the company is struggling financially, but that hasn't stopped the young Crouches from owning eight cars, including a Bentley worth nearly a quarter of a million dollars, and a Hollywood mansion (not to mention the use of TBN-owned real estate in four other states).[12]

In 2003 Gener8Xion Entertainment was engaged in a joint venture with Joseph Medawar, who swindled investors out of $5.5 million to invest in a project to produce a television program about born-again Christian agents at the Department of Homeland Security. A year later, Medawar had pleaded guilty to twenty-three counts of fraud, conspiracy, money laundering, and tax evasion, and his plan to produce a TV series was exposed as nothing more than a sham. But before his efforts were promoted on TBN by both the Crouches and Doug Wead's friend Benny Hinn, Medawar had doors in Washington opened to him by Congressman Dana Rohrabacher (R-CA), a frequent guest on the network.[13] While Medawar was using the TBN airwaves—particularly Hinn's program—to promote his nonexistent television series, Rohrabacher sold a screenplay he wrote in the 1970s to Medawar for $23,000, and Medawar donated $2,000 to Rohrabacher's campaign. Medawar's indictment alleged that he used money he had scammed from investors to pay for the Rohrabacher script.[14] Rohrabacher received clearance from the House Ethics Committee for the transaction, but he did not reveal to the committee that he was also trying to open doors in Washington to Medawar, who claimed to want insider access to make the television show more realistic. Rohrabacher introduced Medawar to members of the House Homeland Security Committee, including Republican Christopher Cox, who later became chair of the Securities and Exchange Commission, and briefly introduced him to First Lady Laura Bush at a GOP fund-raiser.[15] After Medawar pleaded guilty, Rohrabacher returned the money he received for the screenplay.[16]

Hinn helped Medawar promote his insider access for his alleged television series. In what amounted to a free commercial (provided courtesy of Hinn's tax-exempt ministry) for Medawar's investment scam on Hinn's program in late 2003, Medawar claimed to have a "mind-boggling" number of high-level officials consulting on the project. Medawar discussed his joint venture with Gener8Xion Entertainment and claimed that the television series would be shown simultaneously on secular television and TBN. One of the purported actors for the program, Steve Owens, claimed that he was saved a few weeks earlier on *Praise the Lord* with Matt and Laurie Crouch. And Hinn himself engaged in a little name-dropping—including dropping Rohrabacher's—in touting a party he attended with Medawar that was stacked with "Hollywood stars" and "government officials." The theme of the program, Medawar claimed, was to show how Christians can prevent terrorism.[17]

The theme of Christians saving the world from terrorists was repeated, oddly enough, in the promotion of Gener8Xion Entertainment's 2006 film, *One Night with the King*. For the film, based on the biblical story of Queen Esther, the Crouches enlisted not only the free airtime on TBN but also its close ties with conservatives and Republicans in promoting it.[18] Tommy Tenney, the evangelist influenced by Mark Hanby, wrote the book and co-wrote the screenplay for the film. Tenney's ministry had received $16 million from TBN, and he in turn hired Gener8Xion Entertainment to produce the film.[19] Tenney was on hand at the Family Research Council's Values Voters Summit in September 2006, which was also attended by many of the major 2008 Republican presidential hopefuls, promoting the movie as part of a panel on the rising influence of Christians in Hollywood. The film was hyped on TBN for weeks before its release, and Copeland, Hagee, Falwell, Long, Joyce Meyer and other evangelists provided their stamps of approval. The network also gave

money to the Arrow Project, a Texas foster child charity with ties to
Tom DeLay, to offer free screenings of the film to its children.[20]

The movie conveniently dovetailed with the CUFI organizing
principle that Haman, the vizier in the Bible whose plan to wipe out
the Jews was thwarted by Esther, appears again in the form of
Iranian president Mahmoud Ahmadinejad and that modern-day
Esthers must rise to confront him. TBN hyped the idea that *God* in-
tervened on the timing of the film's release, since it had originally
been slated for a 2004 release but experienced repeated production
delays. Jan Crouch effused on the air:

> The Lord began to show me this movie has come for such a
> time as that, that we are living in. . . . God saved this movie.
> We couldn't figure out why it couldn't come out . . . and now,
> right now, just as the king of Iran, the president of Iran, has
> defied the whole UN. Why? Because he doesn't like the Jewish
> people. Is this the most prophetic word? . . . One little orphan
> girl changed the course of the whole Israeli-Jewish nation. One
> can do it. We are one, the Body of Christ. We cannot get the
> Gospel into the beautiful hearts of those Muslim people until
> they realize the Jews are not their enemy. . . . They've got to just
> relax. If people could see this movie and realize that one person
> can make a difference. That's what this movie is about. It's a
> prophetic statement for today.[21]

In an interview at the Values Voters Summit, Tenney claimed that the
prophetic message of the film was more than just about saving the
Jews from modern-day Hamans; it was about reaffirming a fundamentalist reading of the Bible. "The fight is over the land," said
Tenney, referring to Israel. "It's really about the promise that God
said, it would be theirs, and they would continue to exist. And it's
just an attack against God, basically."[22] But people who had seen the
free screening of the movie at the Values Voters Summit didn't seem
to think it was about the Jews—unless that meant converting them to
Christianity. Jesse Edwards, a Pentecostal preacher from Philadel-

phia called the movie "one of the greatest outreach tools of the church in this century," adding that if people "haven't made a dedication to Christ, they will when this is over." And inside the conference, the enemy wasn't Haman or Ahmadinejad but the murky secularists of Hollywood, with whom godly movie producers like Tenney are waging a battle for the hearts and dollars of moviegoers. Just as Tony Perkins, whose Family Research Council organized the event, told Tenney on *Praise the Lord* in 2005 that "government is a mission field," Tenney told the Values Voters Summit audience that Hollywood is a "mission field." What Tenney didn't tell the audience is that the mission is money.

SEVEN

Generation Next

I'm afraid we have people who want to be soldiers
for Christ, but they still have their own identity.
—RON LUCE, at Rod Parsley's
Reformation Generation Conference, May 26, 2007

At Rod Parsley's Reformation Generation youth conference, the first order of business was wringing money out of several thousand kids' hands. The lower portion of the World Harvest Church sanctuary—which Parsley often calls "the tabernacle" in reference to the holy temples of the Bible to which only the high priests had access—was nearly full with teenagers, college students, youth pastors, and a sprinkling of small children, some even of preschool age. Yet while each person had paid $49 ($59 if they didn't preregister) to attend the event, they weren't done handing over their money to their spiritual general. An offering, they were told, was the best evidence that they were committed participants in spiritual battle with Satan, warriors for Christ who had thrown out their own selves so that they could look like "little Christs."

Josh Cossey, the baby-faced, red-headed pastor of Next Harvest, Parsley's youth outreach, called on these Jesus warriors to turn over whatever money they had, even if it was just a quarter. Like the bid for even the tiniest of offerings, the rest of the message was tailor-made for the teenage crowd. Cossey had warmed them up early in the morning by comparing them to John the Baptist, who announced, according to Cossey, "I am here to proclaim to the barbarians to prepare the way for the Lord to come!" But the Second

Coming, it seems, will happen only after a raucous party—*wahoo*—because before Jesus comes again, "it's going to take a generation of John the Baptists, rowdy, crazy . . . to prepare the way for Jesus to return to this earth, in power, in justice, in glory!" Compliantly, the crowd, hooting, shouting, and applauding, repeated after Cossey, "Lord, I'm ready!" and the band played, for the second time, "We Prepare the Way."

Cossey and the other speakers at the conference are programming a generation of "warriors," kids who dress in jeans and T-shirts and wear makeup (girls only) and have cute haircuts and iPods but are armed for battle with their Rod Parsley Breakthrough Bibles, their "No Weapon" backpacks, their "Ref Gen" gear, and "iRod" T-shirts. It's a spiritual battle, they are told, against the big bad world of secularism, run by people who are "vehemently opposed" to the Bible and want to give you condoms and make you think homosexuality is normal. Attending World Harvest Bible College is encouraged to prepare oneself to "invade the culture."

The World Harvest Warriors (indeed, that is the school mascot) aspire to be a resistance movement. But all they are actually resisting is their natural urges—for sex, for exploration, for making mistakes, for being young. And, although they don't seem to realize it or care, they are also resisting a life of curiosity, critical thinking, and well-roundedness. There's not one mention of poverty, corruption, global warming, or other issues at the top of other evangelicals' agenda. Nor, on Memorial Day weekend of the fourth year of the Iraq War, was there talk about the sacrifices and ravages of actual war. The only relevant war was the one they could fight by not thinking about sex; by mocking gay people; by not watching the perniciously omnipresent MTV; by being "a love slave to Jesus"; and, most important, by understanding that the best proof of their virtue was turning over their money to Rod Parsley.

Cossey compared the generation sitting before him to Paul and Silas, who were imprisoned for preaching the Gospel. Playing into the narrative so deftly manufactured by propagandists like Parsley and the conservative media, Cossey claimed Christians are "persecuted" by the "secular culture." But Cossey added another twist—again, custom-made for the teenaged crowd—that Paul and Silas were outcasts. "They have been made fun of at school, and they don't care," he says. Why are the metaphorical Paul and Silas made fun of at school? Because they won't indulge in that dreaded secular culture, which Cossey and the other speakers seem to think is best exemplified by MTV. In fact, the term "MTV culture" is thrown around as if one's only choices were between "spiritual warfare" and watching MTV. It's as if art, literature, other kinds of music, sports, or any other wholesome activities could never function as a reasonable diversion from the devil.

The agricultural metaphor of the Word of Faith movement pervades Cossey's plea for money. He discovered, he said, that at the farm next door to the church sometimes the farmers work at night. But while to an adult audience Word of Faith preachers promise financial abundance in exchange for money, to these teenagers Cossey promises a reward of freedom from secularism for sowing their seed during the metaphorical night. He declares, "We're going to receive an offering right now in the middle of a dark culture." Who is the real battle commander and what does he want? It's Parsley, and the "other generals like our pastor have given us a gift of faith, of seed faith." If you don't "sow," it means you have "allow[ed] the enemy to come in and say, you know what, there's no need to sow." Cossey doesn't care if you're out of money or money's short. "Learn to give . . . because if we don't learn to give . . . we will never learn to receive." Cossey is laying it on thick, forcing three thousand teenagers to wave their offerings in the air. "I want every person in this place, *right now,* to get something in their hand, and I want you to put it in the air real high. It's important, it's important, it's not about anything else, but we're in darkness and we have the light! . . . Darkness is being invaded with light. . . . With your hand up, go, 'We are no longer afraid of the MTV culture. . . . Father, we hold our gifts up in the air. And in the middle of the darkness, we give you light.'"

Cossey was just a warm-up for the main attraction, Ron Luce, president of Teen Mania Ministries. Luce is an energetic forty-something who travels the country speaking to crowds of teenagers, demanding that they give up their MTV and brand themselves with Jesus. Luce is old enough to be the kids' dad (and is in fact the father of teenagers) yet maintains enough up-to-date exuberance to portray himself as the pious yet hip father figure offering up life lessons as powerful as Jesus' parables. Through Teen Mania, Luce hosts Acquire the Fire (ATF) festivals throughout the country, in some cases drawing crowds of sixty thousand to hear what he calls his "Battle Cry" movement. On the surface, ATF looks like a Jesus-palooza that combines Christian rock, dramatic performances, and clean fun for teenagers. But the reality is that ATF is quintessential neo-Pentecostalism: a battle with the devil, dressed up in the worldly pleasures of consumerism, marketed by an authoritarian father figure who demands obedience. In that battle, kids are indoctrinated to believe that they should not only consume Jesus but be consumed by him, until they become one. In Luce's words, they should look so much like Jesus that people will mistake them for him.

As the Christian youth movement grows and multiplies, it provides the most striking evidence of the mainstreaming of Word of Faith teaching. At Parsley's Reformation Generation conference, Luce exhibited his charismatic roots by disparaging "boring" church (meaning traditional, denominational services) and portraying the charismatic church as cool, chic, and thrilling. (He nonetheless welcomes all denominations into his Battle Cry movement.) Luce has finished his stump speech to kids on how they need to lose their identity—like you would if you joined the military—and get "branded" by Christ. "Are you willing to do as Paul did?" he asks. During his ceremony, repeated at every ATF event, kids write down brands they pledge to discard on a piece of paper. Luce ordered them to throw out "drugs, condoms, or other secular stuff" and instead "clothe yourself with Christ." He told them to declare, "I clothe myself in Christ. I only care that people see him in me." After all the kids walked up to the altar and threw their pieces of paper on it, the whole church prayed for Luce, making sure to include prayers for "financial increase" in his family.

Luce maintains close ties with practitioners of the Word of Faith teaching. He graduated from Oral Roberts University in 1983 and launched Teen Mania Ministries in Tulsa before moving it to eastern Texas. I had seen Luce at the ATF event at his old stomping grounds in early 2007, where he was hosted by Billy Joe Daugherty, whose massive Word of Faith Victory Bible Church sits directly across the street from the ORU campus. Seven thousand kids descended on ORU's Mabee Center arena and were greeted by Luce and his traveling band of Jesus warriors, as well as by ORU president Richard Roberts. ORU, Luce told the crowd, "totally changed my life."

At the Tulsa event, it was evident that Word of Faith has already permeated Luce's Christian youth movement, particularly in its use of positive confession and seed-faith theology. One band, Unhindered, repeatedly sang a song that implored Jesus to "consume me from the inside out" and asked him to "teach my lips to glorify you." The band's lead singer told the crowd how "God has spoken the world into existence," one of the main tenets of positive confession. And when the offering was taken up for Teen Mania's Global Expeditions, which sends teenage missionaries around the world, Mike Cuzzardo, an alumnus of Teen Mania's Honor Academy, employed standard Word of Faith buzzwords to encourage kids to turn over their addresses, phone numbers, and e-mail addresses, as well as to donate cash. While they were filling out their cards, Cuzzardo told them to say, "I'm willing to sow my card into someone's life." While collecting the money, he promised that they would see the "first fruits" of "sowing into your peers."

At the Honor Academy, interns "take a year off of their life to passionately seek out Jesus Christ, really connect with him, and build up their own convictions in their own heart about their life," said Nicholas Hart, a twenty-four-year-old graduate of the Honor Academy who stayed on as a call center supervisor for Global Expeditions. But while Hart says interns at the Honor Academy are "passionately seek[ing] Christ," journalist Jeff Sharlet, who spent a week at the academy, described it more as a boot camp, with predawn wake-up calls, classes focusing on obedience and purity, sleep-deprived emotional endurance tests, and enforcement of pledges never to criticize the Academy or portray the ministry "in a negative light."[1]

Hart said the interns use those addresses and phone numbers to solicit more cash. The ultimate goal, said Hart, is "to build up leaders for this generation," leaders who "are gonna go out there and become youth pastors and become doctors and all these kinds of people and just go out there and be this front of this new generation passionately seeking Jesus Christ." It's not clear what all that passionate seeking yields, except more people who want Jesus to consume them, conquer the world, and give money back to Teen Mania. The Honor Academy aims to cultivate leaders of "the United States or even the world." Former Honor Academy interns, Hart said, were serving at the White House, and one had run for governor. And for money, Hart said, "We want to build up leaders who are gonna say, 'Hey, you know what, if God has called me to make a lot of money in my lifetime, I'm gonna be able to sow it back into Teen Mania Ministries and the Battle Cry to support this generation in the things that they're gonna need to do."[2]

Parsley's youth conference was a marketing tool not just for Luce but for his own World Harvest Bible College (WHBC), which is not really a college in the traditional sense but a training ground as pioneered by Hagin and which is slickly presented as "where the word gets real." At WHBC, students are encouraged "to view spiritual conflict as part of daily life," to understand "spiritual authority" and "submission" in ministry, and especially to be able to "recognize the attributes and manifestations of rebellion and the spirit of submission."[3] One doesn't even have to enroll at the school to purchase videotapes through a correspondence program, which includes standard Word of Faith topics like "Seedtime Harvest," "God's Power for Your Prosperity," and "Kingdom Dominion—Your Right as a Believer."[4] The college isn't the only training ground, though; Parsley and most other Word of Faith teachers start early, attaching nursery school through high school to their churches, creating a generation completely inculcated in Word of Faith doctrine.

After Parsley's Reformation Generation had obeyed Luce, discarded their secular brands, and branded themselves with Jesus, they poured out of the church to eat lunch. Local restaurants had set up catering trucks, and people started forming long lines on the steaming blacktop to buy barbeque, taquitos, and hamburgers. Would I see Jesus in the crowd? Was Jesus the blue-haired young woman ahead of me at the barbeque stand who had traveled from North Carolina with her church's youth group because Rod Parsley was her pastor's "spiritual dad"? That Jesus backed away and lost interest when she found out I wasn't involved in a church.

With my barbecue sandwich, I strolled over to the south parking lot to see the Psycho Bike Stunt Team, the lunchtime entertainment that had drawn a large and admiring crowd. I didn't see Jesus there, either, because I, along with a few other people, ran as fast as I could to avoid being enveloped in a cloud of toxic smoke. The bikers, front wheels in the air, were gleefully grinding the back wheels of their cycles into the pavement. Perhaps if Jesus does return to earth, he will not arrive riding a white horse but doing wheelies on a Kawasaki.

CONCLUSION

Victory Is at Hand

The average church member in America gives only
about 2.6 percent of family income to the local
church. . . . The numbers tell a shameful story—
as the average income of Americans has increased,
their spending on anyone but themselves has
plummeted. I am compelled to ask: How is God
going to use us to impact a generation if He can't
even get us to be obedient with finances?

— ROD PARSLEY, *Culturally Incorrect:
How Clashing Worldviews Affect Your Future*

Although the Word of Faith movement is large, growing, and increasingly influential, it remains invisible to virtually everyone I
know. Yet as I discovered in my research and travels to Word of Faith
events, the movement has transformed the nation's spiritual and political character by creating its own insulated media universe. Books
by its most popular proponents sell millions of copies. Many are advertised in *Charisma*, a monthly magazine that claims a circulation of
250,000—roughly the same as the *Nation, Mother Jones,* or *Harper's*.
Every Sunday, the movement's top preachers speak to live audiences
that dwarf those for presidential campaign events and NBA playoff
games. But even those numbers pale in comparison to the audiences
reached every day by the movement's radio and television broadcasts. TBN, the largest religious television network in the world,
claims to reach ninety-two million American households as well as

every major continent through forty-seven satellite providers and over twelve thousand television and cable affiliates.

The movement's message, delivered with pitiless repetition, is victory. Believers will be victorious in all matters, spiritual and financial, and in all battles with Satan, including the final one. Since they're told not to believe what they hear from the news media, they reject information that challenges that message. Their money is perpetually needed both to vanquish Satan and to support the preachers, who, as the tax-free money rolls in, hold themselves up as exemplars demonstrating the success of their own prescriptions. To believers, those prescriptions become ever more enticing as their economic and educational opportunities diminish.

Obedience, followers are told, is required to achieve that victory. By coercing congregants to tithe, convincing them that questioning the pastor represents a "rebellious spirit," or portraying all political disputes as "spiritual warfare" between godly forces and those of Satan, Word of Faith preachers have cultivated an aura of untouchability. Authoritarianism, not democracy, is the guidepost in their churches.

As these preachers have reached into the world of politics, they expect the same rules to apply. Their alliance with the Bush-Cheney regime, where critics are silenced or punished, seems a perfect fit. But the movement's alliance with Republicans will endure far beyond Bush's last day in the White House. As Republican candidates seek the imprimatur of evangelical leaders, many will court the prosperity stalwarts for their ability to reach their large, growing, energetic, and obedient flocks.

Because of their flamboyance, secrecy about money, and apocalyptic worldview, some televangelists have had a rude awakening in the political world. But in the face of criticism or scandalous revelations, they turn to their old bags of tricks. Media exposés of their fund-raising practices, lavish spending, or bizarre policy prescriptions are brushed off, ignored, or condemned as the work of Satan.

Anyone who accuses the anointed Paul Crouch of being a homosexual is straight out of hell—or is headed there. Their solution is to denounce any negative coverage as the evil workings of the "secular media," or to silence reporters.

As a card-carrying member of the secular media, I was ejected by Hagee's security personnel from the 2007 Christians United for Israel Summit in Washington, D.C., after asking an unwelcome question. I had been given press credentials to cover the conference by CUFI's public relations firm, which quickly realized that throwing me out of the conference would not result in the type of press coverage they were seeking. But the message from CUFI's public relations flack was clear: Hagee, he told me, had not been pleased with my coverage of him.

Such behavior is of no consequence to Hagee's followers, just as media exposés of Crouch, Hinn, Parsley, and others have failed to diminish their standing in their supporters' eyes. Because its followers are taught to view the world through a prism of spiritual warfare, the movement endures any scandal. Accusers are satanic, newspapers are contrary to God's word, and critical thinking is denounced. No amount of proof is sufficient to condemn God's anointed ones. Revelation knowledge is superior to evidence that can be seen and heard.

As Word of Faith leaders continue to be extolled as prophets, Republicans continue to find an audience favorably disposed to their central economic principles: denigration of a government safety net, a business environment free of government regulation, and the primacy of the individual over the community. The Word of Faith movement plays on people's economic dreams, which are left unfulfilled by Republican economic policy. Through its central promise—that an investment in the ministry of a Word of Faith televangelist will yield a supernatural return—the prosperity gospel offers a faith-driven business opportunity, one with no prospectus, no accountability, and, because of the status of churches, no regulation.

The systematic undermining of government function—whether through tax cuts to the superrich at the expense of programs to the poor, the Bush administration's and DeLay-run Congress' rampant cronyism and corruption, the privatization of war, or the bureaucratic collapse in the wake of Hurricane Katrina—causes no unease. Welfare is satanic, and only "patsies" would go on the dole. Real men tithe, and the faithful prosper.

As the government safety net has been dismantled by Republican rule and "faith-based initiatives" are vaunted as a better alternative, followers of the prosperity gospel really do have nothing but their faith to rely on. Economic failures in their lives are not the result of bad policy, bad luck, or an unjust distribution of wealth. If only they had been more obedient—and made more supernatural investments—they would have been victorious.

For Republicans, Word of Faith is a faith-based initiative par excellence. As is evident in the cradle-to-college education available at many of the Word of Faith churches and through the networks of television, concerts, conferences, books, and online media, a new generation is always under development. Its leaders are willing foot soldiers in a much-needed get-out-the-vote drive every election cycle. As their celebrity expands, these preachers are a gift that keeps on giving. And every new generation is being taught to obey its leaders' commands to pray, to pay, and to vote.

No one should expect this movement to collapse, or even falter, anytime soon. Disciplined, resilient, impervious to setbacks, and determined to succeed, it will continue to make its mark on American politics and the culture at large.

Notes

Introduction

1. Shayne Lee, *America's New Preacher: T. D. Jakes* (New York: New York University Press, 2005), p. 35.

2. Sarah Posner, "With God on His Side," *American Prospect*, November 2005.

3. *Spirit and Power: A 10-Country Survey of Pentecostals*, The Pew Forum on Religion and Public Life, October 2006, pp. iii-iv.

4. Ibid., pp. iii, 29.

Chapter 1

1. TBN, *TBN Newsletter*, September 2000, available at http://www.tbn.org/about/newsletter/0009/0009indx.htm.

2. Despite repeated requests to his spokesperson, Parsley would not turn over medical documentation he claimed to have of the alleged healing.

3. Thomas Edsall, "The GOP's Brownout," *National Journal*, September 1, 2006, http://election.nationaljournal.com/features/090106njpolitics.htm.

4. "The 50 Most Influential Christians in America," *Church Report Online*, January 2007; Religion News Service, "Religion News Service Spotlights 10 Influential GOP 'King Makers,'" press release, April 18, 2007.

5. *Praise the Lord*, TBN, November 28, 2006.

6. Karen Jensen, author's interview, March 4, 2007.

7. Rod Parsley, *God's Answer to Insufficient Funds* (Columbus, OH: Results Publishing, 1992), pp. 40, 55; Posner, "With God on His Side."

8. John Hagee, *Take America Back* (San Antonio, TX: John Hagee Ministries, 1996), p. 2.

9. D. R. McConnell, *A Different Gospel*, 3rd ed. (Peabody, MA: Hendrickson Publishers, 2004), chapters 6–10.

10. Robert M. Bowman Jr., *The Word-Faith Controversy* (Eugene, OR: Baker Books, 2005), pp. 47–48.

11. Steven Winzenburg, "TV Ministries Use of Air Time, Fall 2004," Grand View College, Des Moines, IA, http://faculty.gvc.edu/swinzen burg/tv_ministries_study.pdf, p. 47.

12. Ole Anthony, author's interview, December 6, 2006.

13. Tilton's Web site, www.successinlife.tv.

14. Milmon F. Harrison, *Righteous Riches: The Word of Faith Movement in Contemporary African-American Religion* (New York: Oxford University Press, 2005), pp. 150–51.

15. Lee, *America's New Preacher*, p. 103.

16. Shayne Lee, author's interview, December 21, 2006.

17. Tony Lee, author's interview, February 20, 2007.

18. Melissa Harris-Lacewell, "Black Churches: Liberation or Prosperity?" *Kinetics*, May 11, 2007, http://kinetics.squarespace.com/faith-and-politics/2007/5/10/black-churches-liberation-or-prosperity.html.

19. Doug Wead, author's interview, March 16, 2007.

20. Ibid.

21. Ibid.

22. Charles A. Shepard, *Forgiven: The Rise and Fall of Jim Bakker and the PTL Ministry* (New York: Atlantic Monthly Press, 1989), p. 223. Jim Bakker, the notorious televangelist, helped Paul Crouch launch the Trinity Broadcasting Network and later went on to launch his own PTL Network until he was exposed in 1987 for paying hush money to a former employee who said he raped her. Preaching a prosperity message on his *People That Love* program, Bakker raised millions but in 1989 was convicted of tax evasion, fraud, and racketeering. Although Bakker alluded to prosperity and material blessings, he was not as ex-

plicitly a Word of Faith teacher as Copeland was. Lee, *America's Preacher*, p. 102.

23. Ole Anthony, author's interview, December 5, 2006.

24. Doug Wead, "Targets: The Vice President and Evangelical Leaders of Influence," memorandum, December 28, 1985, p. 15.

25. Ibid., p. 19. James Dobson was also a "spare tire," as was popular televangelist Oral Roberts.

26. Ibid., pp. 25–38.

27. Doug Wead, author's interview, April 12, 2007.

28. An undercover investigation at the offices of the direct mail firm Response Media of Tulsa, Oklahoma, shows its president, Jim Moore, boasting of the work he did for both Tilton and the Bush campaign. Moore also claimed Tilton "is cleaner than anyone out there." Video, August 26, 1991, provided by the Trinity Foundation.

29. George Bush and Doug Wead, *George Bush: Man of Integrity* (Eugene, OR: Harvest House Publishers, 1988), pp. 31–47.

30. Carlton Pearson, author's interview, February 14, 2007.

31. Doug Wead, memo to George W. Bush and Karl Rove, no date, p. 3.

32. Carlton Pearson, author's interview, February 14, 2007.

33. Doug Wead, author's interview, March 16, 2007.

34. Doug Wead, memo to George W. Bush, March 17, 1998, p. 9.

35. Justin Osteen's Web site, http://www.cwd.com/joa/.

36. Shayne Lee, author's interview, December 21, 2006.

37. George Walker Bush and Karen Hughes, *A Charge to Keep* (New York: William Morrow, 1999), p. 1; David Kuo, *Tempting Faith* (New York: Free Press, 2006), p. 114.

38. Michelle Vu, "Obama Points to Rick Warren, T. D. Jakes as Models for Faith-Driven Action," *Christian Post*, June 25, 2007.

39. Hagee's anxiety about the Council on Foreign Relations reflects the view that led to the formation of the influential and secretive Council for National Policy, founded by Hagee's friend Tim LaHaye. The CNP, made up of the most influential members of the conservative movement, including elected officials, meets in secret three or four times a year. Its support is considered essential for Republican presidential candidates.

40. John Hagee, *Day of Deception* (Nashville, TN: Thomas Nelson, 1997), pp. 39–64.

41. Bush and Wead, *George Bush: Man of Integrity,* pp. 20–21.

42. Hagee, *Day of Deception,* p. 38. Hagee insisted that Bush's reference to a "new world order" in his 1991 speech launching the first Persian Gulf War was evidence of his fixation with instituting a one-world government led by the satanic United Nations. Ibid., p. 43. Hagee continued to harbor resentment toward Baker in the latter's role as chairman of the Iraq Study Group, labeling him "anti-Israel." CUFI Membership Update, e-mail, December 11, 2006.

43. Documents provided by Wead; Kuo, *Tempting Faith,* p. 125.

44. John Hagee, *God's Candidate for America* (San Antonio, TX: Global Evangelism Television, 2000), p. 191.

45. *JHMagazine,* vol. 14, no. 4 (July/August 2002), contained promotional material about the book.

46. Hagee, *God's Candidate,* pp. 185–86.

47. Global Evangelism Television, Internal Revenue Service Form 990, pp. 4, 27. Tax returns of nonprofits are available to the public.

48. Hagee, *God's Candidate,* p. 149.

49. Ibid., p. 147.

50. Ibid., p. 182.

51. Word of Faith followers, particularly of Parsley's and Crouch's generations (Parsley is in his fifties and Crouch is in his seventies) trace their religious roots to Pentecostal denominations like the Assemblies of God. For the Pentecostal roots of Word of Faith, see chapter 2.

52. Doug Wead, memorandum to George W. Bush, October 25, 2000.

53. Doug Wead, memorandum to George W. Bush and Karl Rove, July 18, 2000.

54. Ibid., August 20, 2000.

55. Ibid., August 22, 2000.

56. "U.S. Attorney General, John Ashcroft, Greeting Paul Crouch," *TBN Newsletter,* July 2001, http://www.tbn.org/about/newsletter/0107/index.htm.

57. "Paul Crouch Meets Attorney General John Ashcroft," *TBN*

Newsletter, January 2002, http://www.tbn.org/about/newsletter/
0201/020109.htm.

58. *Behind the Scenes*, TBN, February 27, 2002.

59. "Paul Interviews Congressman Randy Cunningham," *TBN Newsletter*, January 2000 http://www.tbn.org/about/newsletter/
0001/0001indx.htm.

60. *Behind the Scenes*, TBN, August 9, 2004.

61. Anne Coulter, interview, *Behind the Scenes*, TBN, October 20, 2004.

62. John McCain, interview, *Behind the Scenes*, TBN, March 21, 2007.

63. Doug Wead, memorandum to Karl Rove and George W. Bush, July 29, 1998, p. 4.

64. Copeland, through a spokesperson, declined an interview request for this book on that basis.

65. Doug Wead, memorandum to Ophelia Banenbosch (Gov. Bush's assistant), enclosing the book from Copeland, May 16, 1999.

66. Stephen Mansfield, *The Faith of George W. Bush* (Lake Mary, FL: Charisma House, 2004), p. 111.

67. Wead, memorandum to Bush and Rove, August 22, 2000.

68. "Confident Candidate Keith Butler Predicts a 2006 Senate Victory," Eastside Republican Club, http://www.eastside-republican-club.org/butler.htm.

69. "The Mother Jones 400," *Mother Jones*, 2001, http://www.motherjones.com/news/special_reports/mojo_400/96_prechter.html.

70. "White House for Sale," Public Citizen, http://www.whitehouseforsale.org.

71. Mansfield, *The Faith of George W. Bush*, p. 111.

72. Campaign contribution information from the Center for Responsive Politics, www.opensecrets.org.

73. Citizens for Responsibility and Ethics in Washington, "CREW Files IRS Complaint against Living Word Christian Center," October 17, 2006, http://www.citizensforethics.org/node/18993.

74. Jon Tevlin, "The Kingdom and Power of Mac Hammond," *Minneapolis Star Tribune*, February 11, 2007.

75. Charlie Cook, "Butler's Chances," *Cook Political Report,* May 3, 2005, http://www.cookpolitical.com/column/2004/050305.php.

76. Carlton Pearson, author's interview, February 14, 2007. Ray and Jakes did not respond to interview requests, and Long declined to be interviewed.

77. Shelley Henderson, author's interview, April 6, 2007.

78. William Reed, "Thee of Little Faith: An African American Guide to Faith-Based Funding," *East Texas Review,* May 11, 2006.

79. Shelley Henderson, author's interview, April 6, 2007.

80. Ibid.

81. Charles Dervarcis, "Ohio African-Americans Cast Important Votes in Presidential Election," *Black Issues in Higher Education,* December 2, 2004, citing survey work by David Bositis, senior research associate at the Joint Center for Political and Economic Studies.

82. Shelley Henderson, author's interview, April 6, 2007.

83. Archives of the programs are available on Copeland's Web site, http://www.bvov.tv/kcm/archive.php.

84. WallBuilders Web site, http://www.wallbuilders.com/pastors briefing/briefinginfo.htm.

85. Deborah Caldwell, "The Bush Campaign Has Hired David Barton Who Calls the U.S.A 'Christian Nation,'" Beliefnet, http://www.beliefnet.com/story/154/story_15469_1.html.

86. *Behind the Scenes,* TBN, August 22, 2006.

87. Miracle Healing and Victory Service, New Beginnings Church, Irving, Texas, December 4, 2006.

Chapter 2

1. McConnell, *A Different Gospel,* p. 76.

2. Ibid., pp. 76–77.

3. Karen Jensen, author's interview, March 4, 2007.

4. Bowman, *The Word-Faith Controversy,* p. 94.

5. Jack W. Hayford and David S. Moore, *The Charismatic Century: The Enduring Impact of the Azusa Street Revival* (New York: Warner Faith, 2006), pp. 2–3. Hayford is Paul Crouch's pastor and a spiritual

adviser to many evangelists; he was part of the group that "healed" former National Association of Evangelicals president and Bush White House confidant Ted Haggard of homosexuality.

6. Bowman, *The Word-Faith Controversy*, pp. 36–37.

7. Hendrik H. Hanegraaff, "What's Wrong with the Faith Movement, Part One," *Christian Research Journal*, Winter 1993, p. 16, http://www.iclnet.org/pub/resources/text/cri/cri-jrnl/crj0118a.txt.

8. Hendrik H. Hanegraaff, "Faith in Faith or Faith in God?" *Christian Research Journal*, Winter/Spring 1990, p. 31.

9. Ole Anthony, author's interview, December 2, 2006.

10. Hendrik H. Hanegraaff and Erwin M. de Castro, "What's Wrong with the Faith Movement, Part Two," *Christian Research Journal*, Spring 1993, available at http://www.iclnet.org/pub/resources/text/cri/cri-jrnl/web/crj0119a.html.

11. Hank Hanegraaff, *Christianity in Crisis* (Eugene, OR: Harvest House, 1993), p. 70.

12. Hanegraaff, "Faith in Faith or Faith in God?"

13. 3 John 2 (King James Version).

14. Hanegraaff, *Christianity in Crisis*, pp. 223–24.

15. McConnell, *A Different Gospel*, pp. 174–75.

16. Ibid., p. 179.

17. Joshua Levs, "Profile: Debate among African-American Churches on the Direction of Their Messages," *All Things Considered*, NPR, July 31, 2005.

18. "Fox's Hannity Again Smeared Pastor of Barack Obama's Church as 'Black Separatist,'" Media Matters for America, June 28, 2007, http://mediamatters.org/items/200706280002.

19. Robert M. Franklin, "The Gospel of Bling," *Sojourners*, January 2007.

20. Hanegraaff, *Christianity in Crisis*, p. 39.

21. McConnell, *A Different Gospel*, pp. 56–57.

22. Bowman, *The Word-Faith Controversy*, p. 108.

23. McConnell, *A Different Gospel*, p. 143.

24. The supposed wealth of the Jews, the linking of them with prestigious money interests, is a common theme among end-times prophecy advocates like Hagee, who points to supposed evidence of

Jewish wealth through the ages as proof of their status as God's chosen people. See chapter 4.

25. McConnell, *A Different Gospel,* p. 76–77.

26. Copeland serves as a Texas state director for Hagee's Christians United for Israel and has hosted Hagee numerous times on his program to explain the Jewish roots of Christianity. See chapter 4.

27. Copeland and Hagee appeared at an event marking the four hundredth anniversary of the settlement of Jamestown, the Assembly 2007, the purpose of which was "to see America restored to her original purpose—the propagation of the Gospel of Jesus Christ worldwide!" See chapter 3.

28. Richard N. Ostling, "Raising Eyebrows and the Dead," *Time,* July 13, 1987.

29. Hanegraaff, *Christianity in Crisis,* p. 196.

30. Ibid., p. 205.

31. Kenneth Copeland, *The Laws of Prosperity* (Ft. Worth, TX: Kenneth Copeland Ministries, 1974), p. 79.

32. Ibid.

33. Ibid., pp. 79–80.

34. Oral Roberts, "Tribute to a Heritage of Faith," *Believer's Voice of Victory,* March 2007, p. 14.

35. Rod Parsley, *God's Answer to Insufficient Funds* (Columbus, OH: Resultings Publishing, 1992), pp. 84, 41–42.

36. *Breakthrough,* TBN, July 19, 2005.

37. Service at World Harvest Church, August 28, 2005.

38. Hagee, *Mastering Your Money,* p. 17.

39. McConnell, *A Different Gospel,* pp. 109–110 (emphasis in original).

40. Ibid., pp. 110–11, citing Kenneth Hagin, "The Resurrection," *Word of Faith* (April 1977), p. 6.

41. All quotations from John Hagee, *Mastering Your Money* (San Antonio, TX: Global Evangelism Television, 2003).

42. Benny Hinn, e-newsletter, July 20, 2006, available at http://www.bennyhinn.org/emailletters/enl91prosperity.cfm?emb=443 C136D0865474711664733552211A141C1523600F643751443D0D6D4 F201C034466566878311A1A42311224163C1003073714395C6F.

43. Benny Hinn, e-newsletter, March 22, 2007, available at http://www.bennyhinn.org/yourlife/index.php?option=com_content&task=view&id=1681&Itemid=120.

44. Carlton Pearson, author's interview, February 14, 2007.

45. Sermon given at Potter's House Church, Dallas, Texas, December 3, 2006.

46. Shayne Lee, author's interview, December 21, 2006.

47. Carlton Pearson, author's interview, February 14, 2007.

48. Ibid.

49. Ibid.

50. Ibid.

51. Ibid.

52. Shayne Lee, author's interview, December 21, 2006.

53. Adam Nagourney and Laurie Goodstein, "Mormon Candidate Braces for Religion as Issue," *New York Times,* February 8, 2007, http://www.nytimes.com/2007/02/08/us/politics/08romney.html?ex=1328590800&en=3c8c164179e6c40c&ei=5088&partner=rssnyt&emc=rss.

54. Shayne Lee, author's interview, December 21, 2006.

55. Ibid.

56. Carlton Pearson, author's interview, February 14, 2007.

57. Confidential source, author's interview; Hanby did not respond to multiple interview requests.

58. Confidential source, author's interview; Parsley declined to comment.

59. Mark Hanby, *You Have Not Many Fathers* (Shippensburg, PA: Destiny Image Publishers, 1996), p. xiv.

60. Court records; confidential source, author's interviews.

61. Georgia Supreme Court order disbarring Allison, February 17, 1997. For Hanby's involvement with Allison, corporate records available from the Georgia and New York secretaries of state, and tax-exempt applications and tax returns filed by nonprofits operated by them with the IRS. Allison did not respond to interview requests for this book.

62. David Linkletter, author's interview, February 23, 2007.

63. Eddie Long, interview, *Gospel City,* January 21, 2003, available at http://www.gospelcity.com/dynamic/artist-articles/interviews/16. In

the foreword to Long's 2004 book, *Deliver Me from Adam*, which emphasized kingdom and the need for Christians to live in God's image, not Adam's, Hanby told the story of how he introduced Jakes and Long. Parsley also wrote a foreword to the book, in which he said that it would help the reader discover "how to go from victim to victor, from self-centered to selfless, and from being overcome to being an overcomer." Eddie Long, *Deliver Me From Adam* (Truth Communications, 2004), pp. 1–2.

64. Based on information available from state corporate records and tax returns filed with the IRS.

65. Carlton Pearson, author's interview, February 14, 2007.

66. United Pentecostal Church International Position Paper on Technology, http://www.upci.org/doctrine/technology.asp. There are over four thousand UPCI churches in North America. The organization split with the Assemblies of God in the mid-1940s over doctrinal divisions, including UPCI's rejection of the Trinity and embrace of the Oneness doctrine.

67. United Pentecostal Church International, Position Paper on Modesty, http://www.upci.org/doctrine/modesty.asp.

68. Confidential source, author's interview.

Chapter 3

1. Family Research Council has increasingly reached out to court black conservatives, especially using the talents of Harry Jackson and his vitriolic mentor, antigay activist pastor Wellington Boone.

2. "Leaders Tackle Tough Integrity Issues," *Charisma* magazine, April 2004, http://www.charismamag.com/display.php?id=8683.

3. Janice Rogers Brown, "Hyphenasia: the Mercy Killing of the American Dream" (speech at Claremont-McKenna College, Sept. 16, 1999), cited in "Janice Rogers Brown: In Her Own Words," People for the American Way, http://www.pfaw.org/pfaw/general/default.aspx?oid=12751.

4. "Senators Compromise on Filibusters," CNN.com, May 24, 2005, http://www.cnn.com/2005/POLITICS/05/24/filibuster.fight/index.html.

5. Michelle Goldberg, *Kingdom Coming* (New York: W. W. Norton, 2006), p. 13.

6. Perry F. Stone, *Plucking the Eagle's Wings: Discover America's Amazing Hebraic Patterns and Prophetic Destiny* (Cleveland, TN: Voice of Evangelism, 2001), pp. 229–30.

7. Hagee, *Day of Deception,* pp. 2–4. Hagee maintained, for example, that Hillary Clinton made money in the commodities market on her Tyson Foods investment by employing the same type of "witchcraft" used by Jezebel. Ibid., pp. 14–15. He also suggested, citing right-wing tabloids, that Clinton was, like Jezebel, a killer and murdered Vincent Foster.

8. John Hagee, *Biblical Positions on Political Issues* (San Antonio, TX: Global Evangelism Television, 1992), pp. 64, 70.

9. Revelation 2:20 (KJV).

10. Excerpt from Rod Parsley, *Touched by the Anointing;* also at Breakthrough Web site, http://www.breakthrough.net/nurture_room_text.asp?Id=2.

11. Confidential source, author's interview.

12. Debra Mason, "Safe Sex Booklet Dropped," *Columbus Dispatch,* August 15, 1986.

13. "Abortion Protest Staged by Group," *Columbus Dispatch,* p. 2D, December 31, 1986.

14. Confidential source, author's interview.

15. Amended Constitution and By Laws of Word of Life Church (now known as World Harvest Church), filed as part of Application for Recognition of Exemption with the Internal Revenue Service, July 16, 1985.

16. T. D. Jakes Ministries, videotape, August 18, 2000.

17. The political operations founded by Falwell, Robertson, and Dobson include Falwell's Liberty University, Liberty Counsel (a legal group), and his now-defunct Moral Majority; Robertson's Christian Broadcasting Network, Regent University, the powerful legal group the American Center for Law and Justice, which shares lawyers and television personalities with TBN, and his Christian Coalition; and Dobson's Focus on the Family, Family Research Council, affiliated state groups, and the powerful legal organization the Alliance Defense Fund.

18. House Judiciary Committee Democratic Staff, "Preserving Democracy: What Went Wrong in Ohio," Status Report, January 5, 2005.

19. Harry Jackson, author's interview, September 8, 2005.

20. Ibid.

21. Shelley Henderson, author's interview, April 6, 2007.

22. Center for Moral Clarity Web site, https://www.centerformoral clarity.net/About.aspx.

23. Rep. Walter Jones (R-NC), author's interview, September 7, 2005.

24. Tara McLaughlin, "Paid Trip Offered Face Time for Lawmaker, Controversial Ohio Pastor," Religion News Service, December 1, 2006, available at http://pewforum.org/news/display.php?NewsID=12059.

25. CMC Media Center, https://www.centerformoralclarity.net/PressRelease.aspx.

26. CMC, "Adultery: It Ought To Be A Crime," CMC Updates, http://www.centerformoralclarity.net/Articles.aspx?page=2007013005.

27. Congressman Walter Jones, press release, March 2, 2005.

28. Posner, "With God on His Side" (Roberts conference call, Perry bill-signing); CMC Web site, http://www.centerformoralclarity.net/ (advocacy for Roberts and Alito); Kimberly Reeves, "Perry Schmoozes with Gay Bashers," *Austin Chronicle*, June 10, 2005 (Perry bill signing).

29. Pastors' meeting at World Harvest Church, August 29, 2005.

30. Mark Niquette, "'Let The Reformation Begin': A Call for Converts, Voters," *Columbus Dispatch*, October 15, 2005.

31. CMC, press release, June 5, 2006

32. Jim VandeHei and Juliet Eilperin, "For GOP, A High-Priced Pitch," *Washington Post*, June 16, 2003.

33. Jonathan Weisman, "House GOP Fundraisers Put Price on Honors," *Washington Post*, February 22, 2003.

34. Charles "Rocky" Saxbe, author's interview, September 18, 2006.

35. Ibid.

36. Rod Parsley, *Culturally Incorrect: How Clashing Worldviews Affect Your Future* (Nashville, TN: Thomas Nelson Books, 2007), pp. 89–97.

37. Religion News Service "Religion News Service Spotlights 10 Influential GOP 'King Makers,'" press release, April 18, 2007, http://www.religionnews.com/press02/PR041807A.html.

38. Shelley Henderson, author's interview, April 6, 2007.

39. Texas Freedom Network, "The Anatomy of Power: Texas and

the Religious Right in 2006," p. 8, available at http://www.tfn.org/
files/fck/SORR%2006%20ReportWEB.pdf.

40. For Covenant Foundation's contributions, the foundation's tax
returns are publicly available at www.guidestar.org. Regarding Patrick
Henry, see Andrew Buncombe, "The Bible College That Leads to the
White House," *Independent (UK)*, April 21, 2004.

41. See chapter 1 for a discussion of Barton's involvement in
Republican politics.

42. Silja J. A. Talvi, "Cult of Character," *In These Times*, January 2006.

43. Information on Staffel's involvement is from Texas Freedom
Network, "The Anatomy of Power," as well as from publicly available
documents from the Texas secretary of state. Staffel did not respond
to interview requests. Information on the CEO Foundation's contributions to Hagee's school is available from the foundation's publicly
available tax returns. Hagee's political contributions in Texas are
available from the Texas Ethics Commission Web site.

44. The amounts of Leininger's contributions are available from
Texas Freedom Network, "The Anatomy of Power." For Hagee's state
campaign contributions, see the Texas Ethics Commission Web site.
For his federal campaign contributions, see the Center for Responsive
Politics Web site, www.opensecrets.org.

45. For Hagee's involvement in FreePAC, Dan Quinn, author's interview, April 19, 2006. For the funders of FreePAC, see Texans for
Public Justice Lobby Watch, "'Outing' Who Funds Political Hate
Mongering in TX," March 7, 2002, http://www.tpj.org/Lobby_Watch/
freepac.html.

46. From PAL Foundation tax returns.

47. Travis E. Poling, "Durango Blvd. Core of Hotel Expansion," *San
Antonio Express News*, July 8, 1998 (describing Leininger's involve-
ment); Leah Hicks, "Wingate Inns Set to Enter S.A. Market," *San
Antonio Express News*, February 2, 1996 (describing involvement of
Golden Eagle Investments, which Texas state corporate records show
is held by Scott Farhart, Hagee's brother-in-law and trustee). Hagee,
Farhart, and Leininger did not respond to interview requests.

48. John C. Hagee, *Like A Cleansing Fire* (Old Tappan, NJ: Fleming
H. Revell Co., 1974), pp. 20, 40, 38–39, 75.

49. John C. Hagee, *Take America Back* (San Antonio, TX: John Hagee Ministries, 1996), pp. 1–2, 22, 23, 25, 33.

50. Ibid., pp. 12, 20 (emphasis in original), p. 36 (predicting nuclear war), p. 45 (complaining about gays in the military).

51. *Praise the Lord,* TBN, September 28, 2006.

52. Hagee, *Take America Back,* p. 2.

53. Ibid., p. 19.

54. John Hagee, *Bible Positions on Political Issues* (San Antonio, TX: Global Evangelism Television, 1992), pp. 72–75.

55. Hagee, *Take America Back,* pp. 3–4, 12, 33

56. John and Diana Hagee, *What Every Man Wants in a Woman/What Every Woman Wants in a Man* (Lake Mary, FL: Charisma House, 2005), pp. 17, 77.

57. Ibid., p. 15.

58. John Hagee, speech at the Assembly 2007, Rock Church, Virginia Beach, Virginia, April 27, 2007.

59. John Hagee, *What Every Man Wants in a Woman,* p. 14.

60. Information on Hagee's divorce and remarriage are available from public court and marriage license records.

61. John Hagee, speech at the Assembly 2007.

62. Diana Hagee, *What Every Woman Wants in a Man,* pp. 69–70.

63. Confidential source, author's interview.

64. John Hagee, *What Every Man Wants in a Woman,* pp. 13–14.

65. Kenneth Copeland, sermon from the November 2006 Washington, D.C., Victory Campaign, replayed on his television program, *Believer's Voice of Victory,* February 11, 2007.

66. Kenneth Copeland, speech at the Assembly 2007, April 28, 2007.

67. Ibid.

68. Kenneth Copeland, sermon from the November 2006 Washington, D.C., Victory Campaign, replayed on his television program, *Believer's Voice of Victory,* February 11, 2007.

Chapter 4

1. "And the dragon [Satan] . . . went to make war with the

remnant . . . which keep the commandments of God, and have the testimony of Jesus Christ." Revelation 12:17 (KJV).

2. John Hagee, *The Beginning of the End: The Assassination of Yitzhak Rabin and the Coming Antichrist* (Nashville, TN: Thomas Nelson Books, 1996), pp. 119–28.

3. John Hagee, *Jerusalem Countdown* (Lake Mary, FL: FrontLine, 2006 ed.), p. 192, citing Romans 11:17–21, 25–26.

4. Hagee, *The Beginning of the End*, p. 8.

5. Hagee, *Jerusalem Countdown*, pp. 13., 118.

6. *Believer's Voice of Victory*, TBN, November 14, 2006.

7. Hagee, *The Beginning of the End*, pp. ix-x, 8, 105.

8. Stephen Strang, author's interview, March 27, 2006.

9. George Morrison, author's interview, April 5, 2006.

10. "Bloggers Conference Call with Pastor Hagee," *Israel News: The One Jerusalem Blog*, http://www.onejerusalem.org/blog/archives/2007/01/audio_exclusive_12.asp. Hagee made a similar claim during the Middle East Intelligence Briefing at Cornerstone Church on October 21, 2006.

11. Ole Anthony, author's interview, March 24, 2006.

12. Woodley Auguste, Strang Communications publicist, e-mail to author, April 18, 2006.

13. "Our History," *Israel News: The One Jerusalem Blog*, http://www.onejerusalem.org/blog/index.asp.

14. Joel C. Rosenberg, "Two Great Dissidents," *National Review Online*, November 19, 2004, http://www.nationalreview.com/comment/rosenberg200411190851.asp.

15. American Congress for Truth, "Mission," http://www.americancongressfortruth.com/mission-vision.asp.

16. Hagee, *Jerusalem Countdown*, p. 21.

17. *This Is Your Day*, TBN, March 30, 2006.

18. Ibid.

19. Ibid.

20. CUFI, CUFI Rapid Response Update, e-mail, April 17, 2006 (ellipsis in original).

21. *This Is Your Day*, TBN, March 30, 2006.

22. Seymour Hersh, "The Iran Plans," *New Yorker*, April 17, 2006.

23. Hagee, *Jerusalem Countdown*, p. 19.

24. *This Is Your Day*, TBN, March 30, 2006.

25. Daniel Lapin, author's interview, April 10, 2006.

26. Posner, "Pastor Strangelove."

27. David Brog, author's interview, January 5, 2007.

28. *It's Showtime!* (Parsley newsletter), August 2006.

29. David Brog, author's interview, January 5, 2007.

30. CUFI, CUFI Rapid Response Update, e-mail, July 17, 2006.

31. David Brog, author's interview, January 5, 2007.

32. Ben Lynfield, "Israeli Expulsion Idea Gains Steam," *Christian Science Monitor*, February 6, 2002, http://www.csmonitor.com/2002/0206/p05s01-wome.html.

33. Etgar Lefkovits, "Evangelical Heads Honored for Support," *Jerusalem Post*, December 16, 2006, http://www.jpost.com/servlet/Satellite?cid=1164881922813&pagename=JPost%2FJPArticle%2FShowFull.

34. Sheera Claire Frankel and Gil Hoffman, "Is This the Start of World War III?," *Jerusalem Post*, July 17, 2006, http://www.jpost.com/servlet/Satellite?cid=1150886029334&pagename=JPost/JPArticle/ShowFull.

35. William Kristol, "It's Our War," *Weekly Standard*, July 24, 2006.

36. David Brog, author's interview, January 5, 2007.

37. David Horovitz, "Evangelicals Seeing the Error of 'Replacement Theology,'" *Jerusalem Post Online Edition*, March 20, 2006, http://www.jpost.com/servlet/Satellite?cid=1139395642585&page name=JPost/JPArticle/Printer.

38. CUFI, CUFI Rapid Response Update, e-mail, August 14, 2006, in which Hagee announced the upcoming sermon series.

39. Ibid.

40. CUFI, e-mail to supporters, January 30, 2007; campaign contribution from www.opensecrets.org.

41. Information from the Loeffler Tuggey Pauerstein Rosenthal Web site, http://loefflerllp.com/LTPR/.

42. Ken Silverstein, "Donor Scorecard: Tom Loeffler," *Harper's Magazine*, May 15, 2007, http://harpers.org/archive/2007/05/hbc-90000077.

43. CUFI, CUFI Membership Update, e-mail, February 5, 2007. The CUFI Web site then prominently featured a photo montage of Hagee and Gingrich in front of the Capitol.

44. *Believer's Voice of Victory*, TBN, November 14, 2006.

45. "Praise-a-thon," TBN, April 2006.

Chapter 5

1. Brett Shipp, "Televangelist Couple at Center of Debt Controversy," WFAA News 8 Investigates, May 3, 2006.

2. Benny Hinn Ministries, e-mail, November 29, 2006.

3. Brett Shipp, "Jet Flight Records Spur Copeland Ministry Questions," WFAA News 8 Investigates, February 28, 2007.

4. According to flight records provided by confidential source.

5. Kristy Beach, author's interview, December 17, 2006; narrative written by Beach about her mother's experiences provided to author.

6. Copeland, *The Laws of Prosperity*, p. 67.

7. Rod Parsley, panel discussion, *Larry King Live*, CNN, August 4, 2005, transcript available at http://transcripts.cnn.com/TRANSCRIPTS/0508/04/lkl.01.html.

8. Public documents show that World Harvest Church borrowed money to finance the plane, flight records provided by a confidential source and from www.flightaware.com.

9. Rod Parsley, prepared remarks at a news conference on an Ohio ballot measure, September 27, 2006, available at http://www.centerfor moralclarity.net/pdf/2006-09-27-GamblingStatement.pdf.

10. Michael Johnston, author's interview, January 16, 2007.

11. Tim Wirth, author's interview, January 8, 2007.

12. Ibid.

13. Information available from Hughes's and Parsley's Web sites and from corporate records from the Georgia Secretary of State. Hughes did not respond to a request for comment.

14. Janice Fisher, author's interview, January 3, 2007.

15. Ibid.

16. Ibid.

17. Through his spokesperson, Parsley declined to provide such

details in response to written questions from the author in the fall of 2005; he declined to answer any questions for this book, including questions regarding his fund-raising for Sudan relief.

18. Breakthrough with Rod Parsley, "Free the African Slaves of Sudan!" e-mail, September 26, 2006.

19. Dr. Khataza Gondwe, e-mail to author, April 26, 2007.

20. Rick Ross, author's interview, March 16, 2007.

21. Confidential source, author's interview.

22. Ibid.

23. Ibid.

24. Hagee's salary was available from Global Evangelism Television's tax returns; information on the conversion of his nonprofit to a church is from corporate records available from the Texas secretary of state; and his salary compared to other nonprofit executives is from L.A. Lorek, "Unreasonable Compensation?" *San Antonio Express-News*, August 1, 2004.

25. According to Kinney County land records.

26. According to flight records; Shipp, "Jet Flight Records Spur Copeland Ministry Questions."

27. Posner, "Pastor Strangelove."

28. Documents obtained under the Texas Open Records Act from the Texas House of Representatives and the Kinney County Groundwater Conservation District.

29. Jesse Castillo, author's interview, April 17, 2007.

30. Confidential source, author's interview.

31. Confidential sources, author's interviews.

32. Dale Allison, author's interview, October 3, 2005.

33. Posner, "With God On His Side."

34. Samuel Brockway, author's interview, October 3, 2005.

35. Confidential source, author's interview; neither Hanby nor Allison responded to interview requests for this book.

36. Dennis G. Brewer Sr., author's interview, May 11, 2007.

37. John Blake, "Bishop's Charity Generous to Bishop," *Atlanta Journal-Constitution*, April 28, 2005.

38. According to records obtained from New York and Georgia secretaries of state.

39. Blake, "Bishop's Charity Generous to Bishop."

40. John Blake, " Inspiration: Divine or Online?," *Atlanta Journal-Constitution*, May 12, 2007.

41. Confidential source, author's interview.

42. Confidential source, author's interview.

43. Carlton Pearson, author's interview, February 14, 2007.

44. Proof of Claim filed by Internal Revenue Service on January 3, 2005 in *In re Kingdom Vision Network*, No. 04–25382, United States Bankruptcy Court, Southern District of Florida.

45. Information about the lawsuit available from court records; neither Cline nor his attorneys responded to interview requests.

46. Jay Ramirez, author's interview, February 6, 2007.

47. Confidential source, author's interview.

48. Kingdom Vision Network SB 2/A filing to the Securities and Exchange Commission, July 25, 2001, p. 20.

49. Jay Ramirez, author's interview, February 6, 2007.

50. *Lewis Bungard v. Rodney Lee Parsley et al.*, No. 1994 CV 00162, Fairfield County, Ohio, Court of Common Pleas; *Naomil Endicott v. James Parsley et al.*, Nos. 92 CV 007419 and 95 CV 001144, Franklin County, Ohio, Court of Common Pleas; *Dwayne Endicott v. World Harvest Church et al.*, No. 95 CV 006010, Franklin County, Ohio, Court of Common Pleas.

51. A transcript of the sermon was made a part of the court record in Bungard's case against Parsley.

52. Posner, "With God on His Side."

53. Gayle White, "Sex Charges Cast Pall on Bishop Paulk," *Atlanta Journal-Constitution*, January 29, 2006.

54. Denise Weaver, author's interview, April 1, 2007.

55. White, "Sex Charges"; confidential source, author's interview.

56. Confidential source, author's interview.

57. Johnny Enlow, author's interview, January 25, 2007.

58. Ibid.

59. Ibid.

60. Earl Paulk, *Unfinished Course* (Shippensburg, PA: Destiny Image, 2004), p. 203.

61. Johnny Enlow, author's interview, January 25, 2007.

62. Denise Weaver, author's interview, April 1, 2007.

63. Richard Daigle, "Earl Paulk Denies Sex Abuse Charges," *Charisma*, July 2001.

64. Denise Weaver, author's interview, April 1, 2007.

65. *Mark Hanby Ministries et al. v. Jenevieve Lubet*, No. 1:06 CV 0114, United States District Court for the Eastern District of Tennessee.

66. Denise Weaver, author's interview, April 1, 2007.

67. "Sex for Salvation?" *Paula Zahn Now*, CNN, January 19, 2006.

68. Louis Levenson, author's interview, December 1, 2006.

69. Dennis Brewer; author's interview; Stephen Yaklin, another attorney representing Paulk, did not respond to an interview request, nor did Paulk.

70. Denise Weaver, author's interview, April 1, 2007.

71. Confidential source, author's interview.

72. *Two Men and Their Bibles*, videotape, Earl Paulk Ministries, 1996.

73. Ibid.

74. Carlton Pearson, author's interview, February 28, 2007.

75. Denise Weaver, author's interview, April 1, 2007.

Chapter 6

1. Ministry Watch, "Trinity Broadcasting Network's Coffers Are Overflowing with Cash!" *Donor Alert*, March 12, 2004.

2. Ibid.

3. KDFW-TV, Fox, November 29, 2004.

4. William Lobdell, "Televangelist Paul Crouch Attempts to Keep Accuser Quiet," *Los Angeles Times*, September 14, 2004.

5. Ibid.; see also Affidavit of Ole Anthony, September 24, 2004, available at the Trinity Foundation Web site, http://www.trinityfi.org/press/documentation01.html, which includes copies of the Licciardello deposition and the Brewer letters.

6. William Lobdell, "Pastor's Empire Built on Acts of Faith, and Cash," *Los Angeles Times*, September 19, 2004.

7. Ministry Watch, *Donor Alert*, September 2004, available at http://www.ministrywatch.com/mw2.1/pdf/MWDA_092804_TBN.pdf.

8. Carlton Pearson, author's interview, February 28, 2007.

9. TBN, press release, March 26, 2007.

10. Ministry Watch, *Donor Alert,* April 2007, http://www.ministry watch.org/mw2.1/pdf/MWDA_041607_TBN2.pdf.

11. TBN Praise-a-thon, April 10, 2007.

12. William Lobdell and Stuart Pfeifer, "Deep Pockets Fuel His Hollywood Crusade," *Los Angeles Times,* October 23, 2006.

13. Greg Krikorian and Christine Hanley, "'Producer Gets Access' by Dana Rohrabacher," *Los Angeles Times,* November 4, 2005.

14. Greg Krikorian and Christine Hanley, "Official Tied to Alleged Con Money," *Los Angeles Times,* February 18, 2006.

15. Krikorian and Hanley, "Producer Gets Access."

16. Greg Krikorian and Christine Hanley, "Rohrabacher to Give Back $23,000," *Los Angeles Times,* May 17, 2006.

17. *This Is Your Day,* TBN, November 7, 2003.

18. Sarah Posner, "Jesus at the Movies," *AlterNet,* October 13, 2006, http://www.alternet.org/story/42879/.

19. Lobdell and Pfeifer, "Deep Pockets."

20. *Behind the Scenes,* TBN, August 18, 2006; the Arrow Project places foster children in a planned community run by the DeLay Foundation for Kids.

21. *Behind the Scenes,* TBN, September 14, 2006.

22. Tommy Tenney, author's interview, September 22, 2006.

Chapter 7

1. Jeff Sharlet, "Teenage Holy War," *Rolling Stone,* April 12, 2007.

2. Nicholas Hart, author's interview, March 3, 2007.

3. "Courses," World Harvest Bible College course catalog, available at http://www.worldharvestbiblecollege.org/coursedescription1_19.htm.

4. "External Studies," World Harvest Bible College course catalog, available at http://www.worldharvestbiblecollege.org/external%20 studies1.htm.

Acknowledgments

In 2004 I set out to do something many people dream of but often do not accomplish: change careers. Four people deserve special attention for helping me parlay my skills as lawyer into those of a journalist, and eventually to write this book. John Feffer, in a seminar offered by the National Writers' Union, provided helpful advice to a novice on breaking into political journalism. Paul Waldman, who at the time edited the online magazine *Gadflyer*, published my first two articles and gave me my first blogging platform. Michael Tomasky and Joe Conason, who at the time were the *American Prospect*'s editor and investigative editor, gave me the opportunity to report on Rod Parsley and John Hagee, two of the figures featured prominently in this book. The confidence Mike and Joe had in me, not to mention their inspiration, advice, and friendship, have been crucial. Without them, this book never would have been written.

I am also grateful to the *Prospect*'s Ann Friedman and Sarah Blustain, as well as the former web editor, Sam Rosenfeld, and to the entire *Prospect* staff for their continued interest in and support of my work. My former *Gadflyer* colleague, Joshua Holland, and *AlterNet's* executive editor Don Hazen, have consistently brought my work to their audience. My former colleagues at the *Gadflyer*, especially Cliff Schecter, Tom Schaller, and Sean Aday, have encouraged and inspired me, as have many other editors, reporters, and bloggers.

My editor, Peter Richardson, and publisher, Scott Jordan, at

197

PoliPointPress were enthusiastic early on about this project and have been committed to bringing it to as wide an audience as possible. Peter always provided astute insights and a clarity to the editing process. I am always grateful for my wonderful agent, Liz Trupin-Pulli of JET Literary Associates, for her advocacy on my behalf and years of friendship.

At the Trinity Foundation, Ole Anthony, Pete Evans, and Harry Guetzlaff spent a great deal of time helping me understand the history of televangelism and their investigations into televangelism fraud. The Nation Institute provided generous financial support. Alina Hoffman graciously and accurately transcribed many hours of interview tapes. Michael Cantwell provided helpful legal advice.

Many sources shared personal stories with me—some despite fear and intimidation, and some despite profound religious or political differences. Others welcomed me into their homes or churches. To all of them, I am thankful, because I learned something from every one of them, and my readers will, too.

Finally, family and friends encouraged me and accommodated my chaotic schedule while working on this book, especially my husband, Doug Wolfe, my parents, Rita and Herb Posner, and my sister, Lisa Pafe. Many thanks also to John, Jan, and Jay Wolfe, Ann Keeler and Matt Dinkel, Adele Kimmel, Claudia Cantarella, Anne Joseph, Mike Edson and Leslie Spitz-Edson, Charles Sullivan and Marc Benson, Ray Loughrey and Jim Drummey, Mark Seifert and Jeff Dygert, Vikki Wachino and Dan Byman, Charlotte Cluverius and David Klevan, Stephanie Loughlin and Rob Kaye, Jeannie Engel and Jim Kohm, John Vail and Alison Fields, Sue and Laird Burnett, Laura Rosenthal and Russ Mardon, Martin Dieu and Holly Elwood, my book club, the BCC Giants, and all my friends who inquired about my travels, and those who didn't but who listened with interest anyway.

Index

About the Author

SARAH POSNER is an investigative journalist covering the activities of conservative evangelicals. She has written for *The Nation, The American Prospect,* AlterNet, *The Washington Spectator,* and *The Gadflyer.* She also writes The FundamentaList, which counts down the week's top news about the religious right, for *The American Prospect* Web site (www.prospcct.org).

Other Books from PoliPointPress

The Blue Pages: A Directory of Companies Rated by Their Politics and Practices   Helps consumers match their buying decisions with their political values by listing the political contributions and business practices of over 1,000 companies. $9.95, paperback.

Jeff Cohen, *Cable News Confidential: My Misadventures in Corporate Media*   Offers a fast-paced romp through the three major cable news channels—Fox CNN, and MSNBC—and delivers a serious message about their failure to cover the most urgent issues of the day. $14.95, paperback.

Marjorie Cohn, *Cowboy Republic: Six Ways the Bush Gang Has Defied the Law*   Shows how the executive branch under President Bush has systematically defied the law instead of enforcing it. $14.95, paperback.

Joe Conason, *The Raw Deal: How the Bush Republicans Plan to Destroy Social Security and the Legacy of the New Deal*   Reveals the well-financed and determined effort to undo the Social Security Act and other New Deal programs. $11.00, paperback.

Kevin Danaher, Shannon Biggs, and Jason Mark, *Building the Green Economy: Success Stories from the Grassroots*   Shows how community groups, families, and individual citizens have protected their food and water, cleaned up their neighborhoods, and strengthened their local economies. $16.00, paperback.

Reese Erlich, *The Iran Agenda: The Real Story of U.S. Policy and the Middle East Crisis*   Explores the turbulent recent history between the two countries and how it has led to a showdown over nuclear technology. $14.95, paperback.

Steven Hill, *10 Steps to Repair American Democracy*   Identifies the key problems with American democracy, especially election practices, and proposes ten specific reforms to reinvigorate it. $11.00, paperback.

Yvonne Latty, *In Conflict: Iraq War Veterans Speak Out on Duty, Loss, and the Fight to Stay Alive*   Features the unheard voices, extraordinary experiences, and personal photographs of a broad mix of Iraq War veterans, including Congressman Patrick Murphy, Tammy Duckworth, Kelly Daugherty, and Camilo Mejia. $24.00, hardcover.

Phillip Longman, *Best Care Anywhere: Why VA Health Care Is Better Than Yours*   Shows how the turnaround at the long-maligned VA hospitals provides a blueprint for salvaging America's expensive but troubled health care system. $14.95, paperback.

Christine Pelosi, *Campaign Boot Camp: Basic Training for Future Leaders*   Offers a seven-step guide for successful campaigns and causes at all levels of government. $15.95, paperback.

William Rivers Pitt, *House of Ill Repute: Reflections on War, Lies, and America's Ravaged Reputation*   Skewers the Bush Administration for its reckless invasions, warrantless wiretaps, lethally incompetent response to Hurricane Katrina, and other scandals and blunders. $16.00, paperback.

Nomi Prins, *Jacked: How "Conservatives" Are Picking Your Pocket— Whether You Voted For Them or Not*   Describes how the "conservative" agenda has affected your wallet, skewed national priorities, and diminished America—but not the American spirit. $12.00, paperback.

Norman Solomon, *Made Love, Got War: Close Encounters with America's Warfare State*   Traces five decades of American militarism and the media's all-too-frequent failure to challenge it. $24.95, hardcover.

John Sperling et al., *The Great Divide: Retro vs. Metro America*   Explains how and why our nation is so bitterly divided into what the authors call Retro and Metro America. $19.95, paperback.

Curtis White, *The Spirit of Disobedience: Resisting the Charms of Fake Politics, Mindless Consumption, and the Culture of Total Work*   Debunks the notion that liberalism has no need for spirituality and describes a "middle way" through our red state/blue state political impasse. Includes three powerful interviews with John DeGraaf, James Howard Kunstler, and Michael Ableman. $24.00, hardcover.

For more information, please visit www.p3books.com.

About This Book

This book is printed on Cascade Envir0100 Print paper. It contains 100 percent post-consumer fiber and is certified EcoLogo, Processed Chlorine Free, and FSC Recycled. For each ton used instead of virgin paper, we:

- Save the equivalent of 17 trees
- Reduce air emissions by 2,098 pounds
- Reduce solid waste by 1,081 pounds
- Reduce the water used by 10,196 gallons
- Reduce suspended particles in the water by 6.9 pounds.

This paper is manufactured using biogas energy, reducing natural gas consumption by 2,748 cubic feet per ton of paper produced.

The book's printer, Malloy Incorporated, works with paper mills that are environmentally responsible, that do not source fiber from endangered forests, and that are third-party certified. Malloy prints with soy and vegetable based inks, and over 98 percent of the solid material they discard is recycled. Their water emissions are entirely safe for disposal into their municipal sanitary sewer system, and they work with the Michigan Department of Environmental Quality to ensure that their air emissions meet all environmental standards.

The Michigan Department of Environmental Quality has recognized Malloy as a Great Printer for their compliance with environmental regulations, written environmental policy, pollution prevention efforts, and pledge to share best practices with other printers. Their county Department of Planning and Environment has designated them a Waste Knot Partner for their waste prevention and recycling programs.

 PoliPointPress

BUSINESS REPLY MAIL

FIRST-CLASS MAIL   PERMIT NO. 5   SAUSALITO, CA 94966

**PoliPointPress
PO Box 3008
Sausalito, CA 94966-9988**